THE BEDFORD SERIES IN HISTORY AND CULTURE

Apartheid in South Africa

A Brief History with Documents

THE BEDFORD SERIES IN HISTORY AND CULTURE

Apartheid in South Africa

A Brief History with Documents

David M. Gordon

Bowdoin College

bedford/st.martin's
Macmillan Learning
Boston | New York

For Bedford/St. Martin's

Vice President, Editorial, Macmillan Learning Humanities: Edwin Hill
Publisher for History: Michael Rosenberg
Acquiring Editor for History: Laura Arcari
Director of Development for History: Jane Knetzger
Developmental Editor: Alexandra DeConti
History Marketing Manager: Melissa Famiglietti
Production Editor: Lidia MacDonald-Carr
Production Supervisor: Robert Cherry
Director of Rights and Permissions: Hilary Newman
Permissions Associate: Michael McCarty
Permissions Manager: Kalina Ingham
Cover Design: William Boardman
Cover Photo: (front cover) Republic of South Africa, Johannesburg, Apartheid, Racist
    sign posted on a bus / DE AGOSTINI EDITORE / Bridgeman Images; (back cover)
    Copyright Dennis Griggs / Tannery Hill Studios
Project Management: Books By Design, Inc.
Cartographer: Mapping Specialists, Ltd.
Composition: Achorn International, Inc.
Printing and Binding: LSC Communications

Manufactured in the United States of America.

1   0   9   8   7   6
f   e   d   c   b   a

For information, write: Bedford/St. Martin's, 75 Arlington Street, Boston, MA 02116
    (617-399-4000)

ISBN 978-1-4576-6554-7

Acknowledgments

*Text acknowledgments and copyrights appear at the back of the book on pages 175–76, which
constitute an extension of the copyright page. Art acknowledgments and copyrights appear
on the same page as the art selections they cover.*

Ernest Cole photos appearing on page 51 © Ernest Cole Family Trust and courtesy of
Hasselblad Foundation.

At the time of publication all Internet URLs published in this text were found to accurately
link to their intended Web site. If you do find a broken link, please forward the information to history@macmillan.com so that it can be corrected for the next printing.

Foreword

The Bedford Series in History and Culture is designed so that readers can study the past as historians do.

The historian's first task is finding the evidence. Documents, letters, memoirs, interviews, pictures, movies, novels, or poems can provide facts and clues. Then the historian questions and compares the sources. There is more to do than in a courtroom, for hearsay evidence is welcome, and the historian is usually looking for answers beyond act and motive. Different views of an event may be as important as a single verdict. How a story is told may yield as much information as what it says.

Along the way the historian seeks help from other historians and perhaps from specialists in other disciplines. Finally, it is time to write, to decide on an interpretation and how to arrange the evidence for readers.

Each book in this series contains an important historical document or group of documents, each document a witness from the past and open to interpretation in different ways. The documents are combined with some element of historical narrative—an introduction or a biographical essay, for example—that provides students with an analysis of the primary source material and important background information about the world in which it was produced.

Each book in the series focuses on a specific topic within a specific historical period. Each provides a basis for lively thought and discussion about several aspects of the topic and the historian's role. Each is short enough (and inexpensive enough) to be a reasonable one-week assignment in a college course. Whether as classroom or personal reading, each book in the series provides firsthand experience of the challenge—and fun—of discovering, recreating, and interpreting the past.

Lynn Hunt
David W. Blight
Bonnie G. Smith

Preface

Apartheid, a term coined in South Africa in the 1930s to mean a social and political system of "apartness," has become a universal signifier for racial prejudice and segregation. The point of comparison for myriad forms of discrimination, apartheid, along with German fascism and Soviet and Chinese communism, ranks as one of the most notorious systems of social, economic, and political engineering of the twentieth century. It is often compared with the system of Jim Crow laws that segregated black and white across much of the southern United States. More recently, some use the term to describe legal and political discrimination against Palestinians by Israel. Given the system's notoriety, the fight against apartheid is frequently cited as an inspiration to struggle against other injustices. The international tactics used to combat it, such as sanctions and divestment, continue to be mobilized in human rights campaigns. Despite its historical importance, however, many students struggle to appreciate how apartheid worked and ultimately failed in South Africa. By considering the distinctive rise and fall of apartheid in South Africa, this book enables students of world history to better understand diverse cases of institutionalized discrimination.

The introduction to this volume outlines the history of apartheid, highlights key questions that emerge from decades of historical scholarship, and locates the South African history of apartheid within global histories of discrimination and statutory racism. Historians of South Africa have debated whether the rise and fall of apartheid was linked to abstract forces, such as capitalism, or the actions of individuals in organized social movements and political parties. Scholars have also become sensitive to how South African identities cut across boundaries of race, class, and gender. By drawing on this historiography, the introduction allows students and instructors to appreciate how diverse South Africans made history in the context of broader forces of society, economy, and culture, thereby providing the necessary framework to better interpret the documents that follow.

The documents in Part Two were chosen to enable students to appreciate how different and sometimes disempowered segments of the South African population perceived and developed history in ways that are not always accepted or recognized by elites. Elite perspectives, whether those elites created or fought against apartheid, are presented here as well, including texts from the founding ideologues of apartheid, such as Hendrik F. Verwoerd, and those from its chief opponents, such as Nelson Mandela. The documents balance the voices of these elites with those who are rarely recognized as historical actors.

In order to appreciate the multiple facets of apartheid and the diverse raw materials out of which its history has been crafted, this book collects documents from a range of sources. The Truth and Reconciliation Commission (TRC), for example, which investigated apartheid-inspired violence, provides a rich archive of previously silenced voices, a few of which are featured in this collection. Other unconventional sources, including memoirs, interviews, poems, and illustrations, will further enrich readers' understanding of apartheid. These, like all historical sources, come with their particular interpretive challenges, and students are invited to consider them. The fifty documents are collected in seven chronological and thematic chapters. Each document is headed with a note that describes its context and significance. A chronology, questions for consideration, and a select bibliography can be found at the end of the book.

If one reason to study world history is to challenge dominant understandings of the global past, that history has to be found in local perspectives. A guiding premise of this book is that even while apartheid had international supporters, opponents, and consequences, a rich understanding must begin with apartheid's particular South African history. This volume offers such South African perspectives. Even then there are challenges. It cannot claim to represent all South Africans. However, the sources collected here will help instructors and students understand the views and actions of many South Africans who constructed, resisted, and lived with apartheid. Any one of these voices could be amplified or others added. The aim of this book is only to provide an introduction to the cacophony of South African history; enterprising students will use it as a starting point.

ACKNOWLEDGMENTS

Through their questions, discussions, enthusiasms, and silences, the students in my classes at Bowdoin College selected these documents, tested them, and gave shape to this volume. Thanks are due to the following scholars, who reviewed an early draft of the manuscript: Francis Dube, Morgan State University; Robin Hermann, University of Louisiana at Lafayette; John Edward Higginson, University of Massachusetts Amherst; Tamba E. Mbayo, West Virginia University; Molly McCullers, University of West Georgia; Jeremy Andrew Murray, California State University, San Bernardino; Colin Snider, University of Texas at Tyler; and Michael Vann, California State University, Sacramento. In addition, Anne Mager, Keith Breckenridge, Nancy Jacobs, Evan Haefeli, Allen Wells, and Catherine Besteman read parts of the manuscript and offered advice. Thanks to Mika Matsuno, who found Document 37, and Nancy Jacobs, who made it available. Thanks to Bonnie Smith at Rutgers University for having the initial vision for the book; Jane Knetzger, who stuck with it; and Lexi DeConti, who helped with final revisions and provided invaluable editorial assistance. At Bedford/St. Martin's, I would also like to thank Publisher Michael Rosenberg, Acquiring Editor Laura Arcari, History Marketing Manager Melissa Famiglietti, Production Editor Lidia MacDonald-Carr, Cover Designer William Boardman, and Production Coordinator Nancy Benjamin of Books By Design.

David M. Gordon

Contents

Maps and Illustrations

THE BEDFORD SERIES IN HISTORY AND CULTURE

Apartheid in South Africa

A Brief History with Documents

PART ONE

Introduction: Apartheid in South Africa and Beyond

Apartheid became the official policy of the South African government in 1948.* Many features of it were, however, present in South Africa and in many other parts of the world prior to 1948. Racial discrimination was prevalent in many of the most powerful nations, in particular the European countries that colonized Africa and the Americas. Colonies with European settlers, including the United States, Algeria, Kenya, and Rhodesia, enforced systems of racial segregation and frequently codified them into law. Racist scientific notions like eugenics and racist Christian doctrines like the "curse of Ham," the biblical Noah's curse on the descendants of his son Ham, justified discrimination against those with darker skin. Across the African continent, the British, French, Portuguese, and Belgians formalized such racial beliefs into the foundation of their rule by advocating for the development of African societies along their own "racial" and "tribal" lines. Instead of allowing Africans civil and political rights, colonial administrations gave powers of government to chiefs who ruled according to recently invented and politically convenient traditions. Africans were, in short, deliberately excluded from the European-fashioned civilization that justified domination over them.

---

*This introduction is indebted to the literature indicated in the bibliography at the end of the book. The most important recent synthesis, pithy and controversial, is Saul Dubow, *Apartheid, 1948–1994* (Oxford: Oxford University Press, 2014).

After World War II, several challenges to global forms of discrimination occurred. The end of German Nazism made racial discrimination less internationally acceptable. The scientific and Christian bases of racism were challenged. In addition, ideas of national self-determination, enshrined by the Atlantic Charter, signed in 1941 by the future victors of World War II, inspired African insistence on independence. By the 1950s, when African Americans organized protests against segregation in the southern United States, the struggle against racism became associated with the struggle for African independence. African political elites, alienated from the supposedly traditional rulers supported by the colonial states, demanded political and civil rights. In those African colonies with a substantial European settler class, the struggle against racial discrimination and the struggle for national self-determination most closely overlapped.

Across Africa, therefore, European colonial regimes faced two options after World War II: confront African resistance, sometimes armed, or reform colonialism and accept greater African involvement in government and civil society. Most British and French colonial policymakers chose the politics of reform, which soon led down the path of decolonization and political independence. Those Europeans who had settled in African colonies and formed a racial aristocracy faced the prospect of losing their privileges. Years of fraught conflict between European settlers, colonial reformers, and black Africans followed.

PRECURSORS

In South Africa, European settlers were more dominant than in any other African colony. They were also divided into many groups, but principally between those who spoke Afrikaans on the one hand and those who spoke English on the other. Afrikaans speakers were descendants of the Dutch settlers and persecuted French Protestants, called Huguenots, who fled to the Dutch colony at the Cape of Good Hope in the second half of the seventeenth century. Afrikaans, which became a formal language only in the early twentieth century, evolved since that time through interactions among European settlers, the indigenous inhabitants of the Cape, and imported slaves. Afrikaans speakers of European descent became known as Afrikaners or Boers, meaning "farmers." English speakers arrived after the British took over the Dutch-ruled Cape Colony in 1806, and through the nineteenth and twentieth centuries incorporated migrants from many parts of Europe. Debt and the

British emancipation of slaves in 1834 drove the Boers into the interior, beyond British authority, where they constituted their own "Boer republics," the Transvaal and Orange Free State. When the British sought to extend their administration over these Boer republics following the discovery of gold deposits on the Witwatersrand in the Transvaal, the Boers fought a bitter and protracted anti-imperial war, the Anglo-Boer War of 1899–1902. The British won the war, but the treatment of the Boers, in particular the British scorched-earth policy and the incarceration and death of Boer civilians in British concentration camps, fueled anti-British sentiments and laid the foundation for twentieth-century Afrikaner nationalism.

The British were eager to appease the Boers in the postwar settlement. The priority was national unity—in other words, unity between the British and Afrikaners, achieved on the backs of black South Africans if need be. The South Africa Act of Union of 1909 (implemented in 1910) allowed for white self-rule over the union of the two Boer republics and the two British colonies, the Cape Colony and Natal (Map 1). The Union of South Africa, first led by the moderate Boer generals Louis Botha and Jan Smuts, laid the foundation for white rule over black South Africans.

In South Africa, as elsewhere, racial identities are historical and political constructions. White identity came to encompass not only English and Afrikaans speakers who heralded from the United Kingdom, the Netherlands, and France, but also Jewish people from eastern and central Europe, Greeks, Portuguese from Madeira and Mozambique, and Lebanese. East Asians and some other Middle Eastern populations confounded South African racial classifications: At first many were excluded from being white, but, driven by the apartheid government's need for diplomatic relationships, some of these communities became "honorary whites." The designation "black" is as ambiguous as "white." Typically, "black" refers to indigenous Africans who speak nine distinct Bantu languages and who settled in southern Africa from one thousand to two thousand years ago. The apartheid regime referred to these peoples as "Natives" or "Bantu," terms that are now considered offensive in South Africa; in this volume, they are called "Africans," which is the convention in South Africa today. Sometimes Africans are referred to in terms of "tribes," but this volume avoids tribal classifications because they presume fixed identities that do not match present or past realities. (Such tribal categories were, however, key to apartheid terminology and are an important way that many South Africans identify themselves today.) The mixed-race descendants of mostly non-Bantu-speaking indigenous peoples (the Khoi and San peoples, who lived across southern Africa

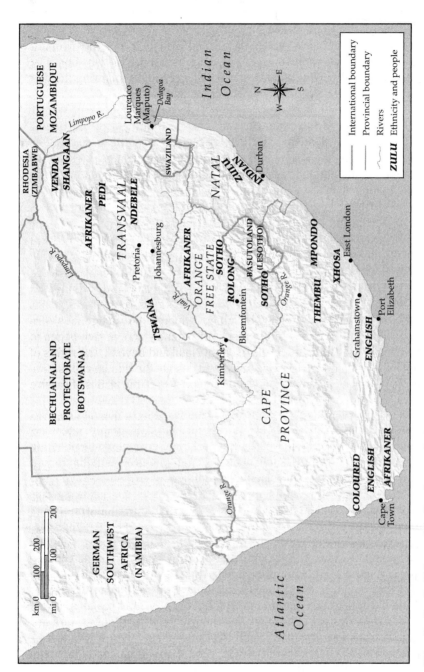

Map 1. *South Africa and Its People, ca. 1910*

4

for many thousands of years), imported slaves, and Dutch farmers are called—and sometimes call themselves—"coloureds." Since they were generally the slaves of Dutch farmers (until emancipation in 1834), most coloureds speak Afrikaans as their first language, although few would call themselves Afrikaners. South Asians, the majority of whom were indentured to work in Natal's sugar fields in the late nineteenth century, formed another major South African population group, the Indians or "Asiatics" (see Map 1 for the approximate locations of South Africa's peoples around 1900). The ambiguity with the "black" label arises from the fact that the South African government—along with many coloured and Indian South Africans—might declare coloured and Indian identities to be "black," even while recognizing that coloured and Indian ancestries and cultures are distinct from Bantu-speaking African South Africans. In short, it is helpful to think of black and white as political identities, each with great variations in culture and history.

In the first decade of the twentieth century, the reconciliation of the Boers and British took precedence over the expansion of rights to all of these black South Africans. Political rights enjoyed by black South Africans in the Cape Colony, including coloured and indigenous Africans, were not extended to the rest of the country and, in fact, began to be done away with in the Cape itself. In Natal and beyond, the rights of Indians were increasingly circumscribed despite the human rights campaigns headed by Mahatma Gandhi, who pioneered his tactics of passive resistance in South Africa.

In this period, the South African economy came to rest on what one scholar has referred to as an "uneasy alliance of maize and gold"—in other words, white farmers and the growing mining industry.[1] White farmers wanted to secure legal tenure over the land they had expropriated from Africans in the preceding century, as well as a cheap labor force to work this land. The profitability of mining deep-level gold deposits also rested on cheap labor. White farmers forced Africans off the land, and both farmers and mine owners benefitted from their landlessness. The law that laid the foundation for this economic system, and ultimately for apartheid, was the Natives Land Act of 1913, which deprived indigenous Africans of 87 percent of the country's land and allotted them the least productive of the remainder (Document 1). Vast parts of the Transvaal and Orange Free State plateau, the Highveld, which included fertile agricultural lands and rich gold and mineral deposits, were restricted to white ownership. The Land Act contributed to landlessness and a cheap, vulnerable workforce. Whether such legislation—and subsequently apartheid in general—ultimately suited the interests of South African capitalism, particularly the mining industry, or only protected white privilege has been a subject of debate among South African historians.[2]

The effects of the Land Act and the new post–Anglo-Boer War dispensation were a great disappointment to the British-educated black elite. They had generally sided with the British during the Anglo-Boer War and hoped that greater political rights would follow. Instead, men like Sol Plaatje witnessed the devastating effects of the Land Act, which Plaatje recorded in his *Native Life in South Africa* (Document 2). Together with other black elites, he formed the South African Native National Congress in 1912 to oppose the Land Act (Document 3). In 1923 this organization was renamed the African National Congress (ANC), the single most important opponent of the future apartheid regime.

White politics from 1910 to 1948 revolved around the pro-British Jan Smuts. There were challenges to him from Afrikaner leaders, in particular, J. B. M. Hertzog, a former Boer general and advocate for Afrikaner nationalism. Hertzog, leader of the National Party, was prime minister of South Africa from 1924 to 1939, at first opposed to Smuts (until 1934) and then alongside him in the United Party (UP). He wanted to promote Afrikaner cultural and national identity, as well as protect white—specifically poor white and Afrikaner—interests. And yet it was Smuts who pioneered some of South Africa's most significant policies until the defeat of his UP in 1948. Smuts developed the segregationist precursors of apartheid, as articulated in a 1917 speech (Document 4). An ardent internationalist, Smuts and his supporters, including President Woodrow Wilson in the United States, were not willing to accept equality between whites and blacks or racial integration. The main political question was how much black involvement should be allowed in "civilized"—meaning for them "white"—society.

Through the 1930s, Afrikaner elites became distrustful of Smuts's close relationship with the British and his lack of attention to Afrikaner interests. This was a heady time for Afrikaner nationalism: Afrikaner cultural organizations emerged; the language of Afrikaans became standardized; an Afrikaans press was established, and an Afrikaner history was taught, commemorated, and ritualized. Afrikaner leaders gathered in a secretive organization termed the Broederbond (Brotherhood, established in 1920), intent on securing the welfare of the Afrikaner nation. For some, Hertzog's alliance with Smuts—and hence with British imperialism—was unacceptable. A Dutch Reformed Church minister and longtime Boer nationalist D. F. Malan formed the Gesuiwerde (Purified)

National Party. Influenced by eugenics and even German Nazism, they sought to ensure racial purity and feared that sexual contact and reproduction between races, so-called miscegenation, would pollute the Boer nation (Document 5). As an alternative to communist influence, which they imagined benefitted from miscegenation, Afrikaner intellectuals envisaged a system of people's capitalism (*volkskapitalisme*), which would improve the lot of Afrikaner capitalists and workers. They also elaborated a system of Christian nationalism as a moral guide for the people. It was in these circles that the term *apartheid* first appeared.

THE IDEOLOGY AND FUNCTIONING OF APARTHEID

In 1939 Hertzog broke with Smuts over his decision to fight alongside the Boers' old foe, Britain, in World War II. Hertzog resigned as prime minister, and Smuts took his place. Hertzog then joined the Herenigde (Reunited) National Party (NP), led by D. F. Malan. The NP appointed the Sauer Commission (Document 6) as an alternative to the United Party's Fagan Commission, which advocated for racial segregation but accepted that white and black existed in the same country and were economically interdependent. The Sauer Commission instead advocated for a policy of "apartheid," which for the first time would promise separate governmental structures for indigenous black South Africans and European-descended white South Africans. Coloureds and Indians would be separated socially and geographically but incorporated into white political institutions, albeit not allotted full political rights. In 1948 Malan's NP rallied behind the slogan of apartheid and defeated Smuts's UP.

Initially, the policies of apartheid were vague. The new NP government was more insistent on segregation and white superiority (*baasskap*) than the UP, but the nature and longevity of this policy were doubted. The NP had won the election by a narrow margin, and members' capacity to mobilize other English-speaking South Africans behind their party was unclear. Moreover, South Africans then, as historians do today, wondered whether apartheid was simply a stricter application of segregation—more continuity than change—or a decisive and novel form of racial, social, and economic engineering, like German Nazism.

Apartheid was closely linked to Afrikaner nationalism. Indeed, since Malan's NP claimed to represent the ideals and interests of Afrikaner nationalism, some historians have seen apartheid and Afrikaner nationalism as being inextricably intertwined. This view needs qualification, however. A few Afrikaner nationalists were not fervent segregationists, and the segregationist discourse taken up by the NP first emerged in British colonial circles. Nevertheless, Malan's NP, and the intellectuals who constituted it, tied the Afrikaner nationalist project to apartheid.

Hendrik F. Verwoerd was the single most important politician in the development of apartheid. He consolidated Afrikaner support for the NP to an unprecedented degree and also mobilized many English-speaking South Africans behind white supremacy. White economic prosperity, along with an extension of the celebration of Afrikaner culture to that of white South African culture in general, helped promote the idea of a white nation. For example, in 1952 whites displayed their unity by commemorating the tercentenary of Jan van Riebeeck, the Dutch East India Company official who established an outpost at the Cape in 1652 (Document 7). He was a relatively neutral figure for white South Africans, remote in time, well before the bitter conflict of the Anglo-Boer War. During apartheid, Van Riebeeck became a national symbol, and his image adorned the South African currency. The date of his settlement became the beginning of the white South African nation. Conversely, black South Africans adopted the same date as the onset of their oppression. In 1966, drawing on such white nation building, Verwoerd could insist that white South Africans shared an identity and had a right to national self-determination (Document 8).

As the minister of Native (African) affairs from 1950 to 1958 and then as prime minister from 1958 until his assassination in 1966, Verwoerd developed the blurred outline of apartheid into a stark political reality. He was responsible for passing the majority of the apartheid legislation (Document 9). The Population Registration Act of 1950 sought to classify all South Africans into one of four racial groups—whites, coloureds, Indians, or Africans—supposedly based on ancestry, but often according to arbitrary criteria. The Bantu Education Act of 1953 restricted the higher education of black Africans by ending independent schools that had educated an African elite and instead providing state education deemed suitable for the "Bantu." This was typical of the prescriptive cultural relativism—that is, the imposition of separate institutions supposedly adapted to separate identities—that came to underpin apartheid.

African citizenship was assigned to separate "tribal" political units. The most important law in this regard was the Bantu Authorities Act of 1951 and the Promotion of Bantu Self-Government Act of 1959, which envisaged separate governments in autonomous or nominally independent "homelands," often referred to as Bantustans (Map 2). Ensuring that blacks would reside in these homelands required the development

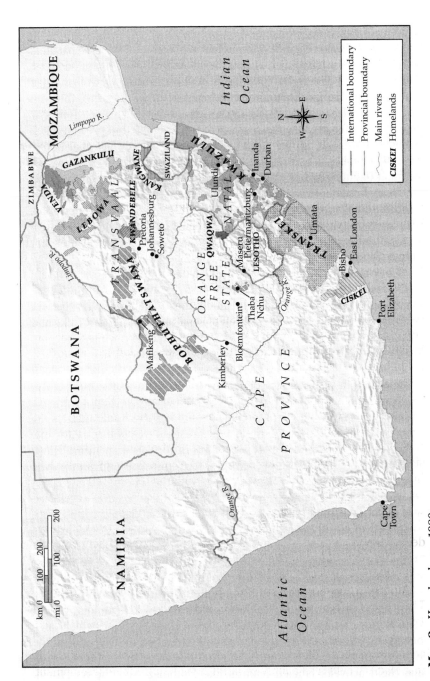

Map 2. *Homelands, ca. 1980s*

9

of controls on the movement of blacks through a comprehensive system of bureaucratic surveillance. Although also a feature of the pre-apartheid segregation era, this form of population control was instituted to an unprecedented degree by Verwoerd's government. An Orwellian-titled law insisted that all Africans carry "passes" in white areas (but not coloureds and Indians), even while it claimed to abolish a previous system of pass control. So-called influx control attempted to prevent black urbanization by permitting permanent residence only in tribal homelands. Such laws constituted the major forms of apartheid's social and political engineering, known as "grand apartheid," or the euphemism "separate development." Saul Dubow points out that apartheid's creation of such ethnic homelands, along with the subsequent population removals, contrasts with other examples of international relocations that generally occur during or after war and that seek to protect minorities, not create them.[3]

Other apartheid laws dealt with everyday forms of separation and segregation, much like the Jim Crow laws of the U.S. South. These "petty apartheid" prohibitions included those against interracial sex and marriage, as well as the creation of separate facilities for blacks and whites. Signs identifying facilities for "whites" and "non-whites" became a pervasive feature of the urban landscape (Document 10).

For apartheid authorities, the collaboration of a section of the black leadership with their vision of separate government was paramount. The Nationalists (the term used to refer to members of the National Party) hoped that they would find supporters among the traditional chiefs, who, in their thinking, were the true representatives of black Africans. Yet chiefs were not enthusiastic supporters of Verwoerd's policies. Those who refused to collaborate were removed from office, and alternatives were found. A group of chiefs went along with the scheme, albeit grudgingly. Chiefs at the upper echelons could use their position to criticize aspects of apartheid, although such criticism was dismissed, as demonstrated in the transcript of a meeting between homeland leaders and Prime Minister B. J. (John) Vorster, in 1975 (Document 12). Gatsha Buthelezi, the "prime minister" of the Zulu, the largest of South Africa's ethnic groups, and one of the most influential collaborators, always insisted on his autonomy from the apartheid government and frequently used his political platform to offer mild rebukes (Document 11). In 1975 he formed the Zulu nationalist organization Inkatha (which later became the Inkatha Freedom Party) in the tradition of ANC opposition. Even so, he was drawn into the system of separate development. Anti-apartheid activists labeled leaders like Buthelezi and the apartheid-sanctioned chiefs "stooges" and "sellouts." Consequently, by the late 1980s, the liberation of South Africa from apartheid involved not only liberation from white supremacy but also a conflict with the chiefs, traditional and otherwise, who retained power over their fiefdoms.

Over nearly fifty years of National Party rule, apartheid evolved from a system rooted in early-twentieth-century segregation to one of political devolution, which its crafters sought to present as consistent with national self-determination and the patterns of decolonization across the continent. White South Africans thought they could coexist as a nation alongside a group of small, dependent African homelands. Through the second half of the twentieth century, the NP attempted to preserve the principle of white supremacy with various federal proposals. The liberation movement, in particular the ANC, consistently opposed them by insisting on equal political rights in a united South Africa.

DEFIANCE: CREATING A LIBERATION MOVEMENT

Just as apartheid became a sign of racial-based rule and segregation, resistance to apartheid became one of the great human rights struggles of the second half of the twentieth century. Resistance to apartheid took many forms, including organized passive resistance, almost thirty years of armed guerrilla struggle, and everyday forms of resistance. Several political organizations and leaders rallied people against apartheid; most dominant was the African National Congress (ANC) of Nelson Mandela.

The attribution of the struggle against apartheid to Mandela and the ANC alone needs to be qualified. Mandela attained much of his reputation as the leader of the liberation struggle during his twenty-seven years in prison following his conviction for sabotage and attempted revolution in 1964. Before then, he had played a key role, but along with several other personalities. In the 1940s, he and other members of the ANC Youth League (ANCYL), including Walter Sisulu, Anton Lembede, Oliver Tambo, and Robert Sobukwe, pushed the ANC in a more radical direction by insisting on popular mass action campaigns instead of the elite lobbying on which the ANC had previously relied (Document 13). It was, however, the charismatic Zulu chief Albert Lutuli who actually led the ANC in the mass campaigns of the 1950s (Document 19).

The central political question within the liberation movement in the 1950s and 1960s was that of alliances between Africans, whites, Indians, and coloureds in the struggle against apartheid. On the one hand, the Africanists of the ANCYL had included coloureds in their definition of African, were unsure about Indians, and were reluctant to include whites. They were suspicious of white communists and rejected an alliance with the South African Communist Party (SACP). On the other hand, an inclusive segment of the ANC argued for a broad alliance of all those who fought against apartheid. Ultimately, in 1959, this led to the most decisive break in the liberation movement, when Robert Sobukwe led some of the Africanists to form the Pan Africanist Congress (PAC) (Document 18). The PAC embarked on a heady campaign of mass resistance, and the ANC had to be careful not to be perceived as a group of out-of-touch moderates who would give way to a more radical nationalist party, as had happened in other parts of British-ruled Africa, such as Ghana, Kenya, and Zambia.

The mass protest campaigns of the 1950s and 1960s defined the rituals, slogans, personalities, and many of the events that became canonized in South African struggle history. The Defiance Campaign, launched on the same day in 1952 that white South Africans celebrated the Van Riebeeck tercentenary, began the ANC's program of mass popular action (Document 14). The spiritual "Nkosi Sikelel' iAfrika" (Lord Bless Africa) became the anthem of the South African anti-apartheid protest movement (Document 16). Call-and-response slogans such as "Amandla Ngawethu!" (Power! It Is Ours!) and "iAfrika! Mayibuye!" (Africa! Let It Return!) became part of popular political performances. In 1955, at the Congress of the People in Kliptown, outside Johannesburg, five thousand delegates drew up the Freedom Charter (Document 17). In 1956 women marched on the government buildings in Pretoria to protest the extension of the pass laws to women, repeating the chant "You strike a woman, you strike a rock" (Document 15).

Such slogans, songs, commemorations, and documents remained part of the repertoire of resistance even as the apartheid state drove the liberation movement underground. The first prohibition against political organizing was the banning of the SACP in 1950. Following the Defiance Campaign of 1952 and the growing mass movement against apartheid, the state arrested black political leaders and tried them for treason beginning in 1956. Even though all were acquitted in 1961, state repression increased through the next decade.

VIOLENCE AND ARMED STRUGGLE

A PAC-led campaign against the pass system changed the nature of oppositional politics. At Sharpeville on March 21, 1960, police opened fire on a crowd of protesters at a PAC demonstration, killing sixty-nine individuals (Document 20). Verwoerd banned the ANC and PAC and declared a state of emergency. Within the liberation movement, the Sharpeville massacre gave legitimacy to those who were already arguing for violent action against the apartheid state, notably Mandela. The ANC and SACP formed Umkhonto we Sizwe (Spear of the Nation), which became known simply as MK, and the PAC formed Poqo (meaning "alone" or "pure").

The first attempts to sabotage economic and military infrastructure had limited success. In 1963 a raid of MK's secret headquarters at a farm in the Rivonia suburb, north of Johannesburg, where a program of sabotage was being planned, led to the arrest of many of the leaders. At what came to become known as the Rivonia Trial (1963–1964), Nelson Mandela, who had been captured the previous year, was convicted of sabotage and attempted revolution along with seven other co-trialists (of ten defendants, two were not convicted). In a famous and eloquent address during the trial, Mandela explained his political goals and why he perceived the need for violence (Document 21). It was his last public pronouncement before being sentenced to life imprisonment. Mandela served twenty-seven years of this life sentence, much of it on Robben Island, a few miles offshore from Cape Town. The other convicted trialists served with Mandela on Robben Island except for the only white trialist convicted, who was imprisoned in Pretoria Central, the only prison for white political prisoners.

State violence and repression increased from that point on. After 1963 anti-apartheid activists could be detained for three months without trial, and torture of these political detainees became common. An elaborate security apparatus was developed, including the infamous Bureau of State Security (BOSS). Such repression crushed the ANC and PAC, and they all but disappeared from the country. Through the next decade, as other political prisoners were sent to "the Island," their isolation from South Africa was complete (Document 23). Among those in exile, there remained much bravado. The ANC proclaimed a violent insurrection led by the people in 1969 (Document 22), even as its structures within the country and its capacity to inflict damage collapsed. A romantic tendency that glorified aspects of the armed revolutionary struggle even filtered up to the sober leadership of Mandela's closest partner, Oliver Tambo (Document 24). This perspective was out of touch with reality in South Africa. Up until the student uprisings of the 1970s, political resistance, armed or otherwise, remained dormant.

RESISTANCE AND REPRESSION: STUDENTS, WORKERS, WOMEN, CLERGY, AND CONSCRIPTS

From the 1970s to the 1990s, the resistance of ordinary people inside the country formed the greatest challenge to the apartheid regime. Students and youth, in particular, reinvigorated the struggle against apartheid. Women, workers, and Christians also linked their own liberation to national liberation.

In the 1970s, black students reignited the struggle against apartheid, with "Bantu education" as their primary complaint. They rallied behind a new ideology, Black Consciousness, as developed by the charismatic student leader Stephen Bantu (Steve) Biko, who was killed in detention in 1977 (Document 25). Students insisted on their black identity and on black agency. They declared that the struggle against apartheid was a racial one, not a class one, as claimed by the communist theory then fashionable in ANC circles. State attempts to introduce Afrikaans as a dual language of instruction (with English) ignited the protests, most famously the June 1976 student uprising in Soweto, the largest township outside Johannesburg, which quickly spread across much of the country. Many students were killed. The photo of young Hector Pieterson, one of the first victims of the uprising, became a symbol of apartheid violence. Even those who photographed the uprising, like Sam Nzima, were hounded by the apartheid security apparatus (Document 26). Student activists were imprisoned or fled into exile, where they reinvigorated the ANC and, to a lesser extent, the PAC.

Struggles over women's liberation and, to a lesser extent, LGBT (lesbian, gay, bisexual, and transgender) rights became entwined with the national liberation struggle. Many women within the Federation of South African Women and the ANC Women's League stood out as leading antiapartheid activists. Yet the ANC leadership structures, along with South African society, remained patriarchal and dominated by men. This contributed to debate among women's rights activists over the relative order and importance of women's versus national liberation (Document 28). A few gay activists, in particular Simon Nkoli, also threw in their lot with the national liberation movement, leading to greater sensitivity toward homosexual rights within the ANC leadership.[4] Through their attachment to national liberation, women and gay activists secured progressive post-apartheid laws, although they were not necessarily matched by changes in the prejudices of South Africans.

The mining industry led to industrialization and to the rise of a unionized African working class. In 1985 thirty-three unions came together to form the Congress of South African Trade Unions (COSATU). COSATU affiliated itself with the ANC and SACP, forming what became known as the Tripartite Alliance. This alliance had both benefits and costs for workers. Workers' rights were linked to the struggle against apartheid. This was a powerful weapon in the anti-apartheid arsenal, since the South African economy could be brought to a standstill by so-called political strikes, as it was on several occasions in the 1980s. However, the success of the liberation struggle did not necessarily mean better wages or improved workers' rights. Union affiliates realized the double-edged nature of the alliance. In 1987, for example, one COSATU-affiliated union, the National Union of Metalworkers of South Africa (NUMSA), criticized COSATU's emphasis on liberation instead of wages and socialism (Document 29). Such critiques were prescient: After apartheid, COSATU members found their bargaining rights compromised by their alliance with the ruling party. In 2014 NUMSA broke with COSATU over this issue.

For much of the first half of the twentieth century, Christian churches, in particular the Dutch Reformed Church, supported apartheid. After the 1960s, however, Protestant and Catholic churches—under the influence in part of liberation theology but also of certain clergy, most famously Archbishop Desmond Tutu—turned decisively against apartheid. In the most confrontational moment, in 1985, churches signed the KAIROS document, which insisted that they side with the oppressed (Document 30). As activists were hounded underground and imprisoned, clergy galvanized the mass movement against apartheid. Church-led funerals of activists became emotional highlights in the repertoire of resistance.

Black South Africans, including coloureds and Indians, formed the overwhelming majority of both the activists against apartheid and the victims of it. White society was divided as well. In the 1950s and 1960s, many white opponents of apartheid were also members of the SACP, such as the apartheid regime's devil incarnate and liberation movement's hero, Joe Slovo. Some liberals, such as the indefatigable member of parliament for the wealthy English-speaking white suburb of Houghton (Johannesburg), Helen Suzman, opposed apartheid from within parliament. By the 1980s, young white South Africans began to reject apartheid. For wealthy English-speaking whites, the vocal rejection of apartheid entailed no great discomfort and was rather fashionable. The break with apartheid among Afrikaners, however, involved a greater existential dilemma. Those who paid the highest price were conscientious objectors, young white men who either refused to be conscripted into the apartheid army, the South African Defence Force (SADF), or deserted it (Document 33).

In 1983 workers, students, clergy, conscientious objectors, and other activists joined in the multiracial United Democratic Front (UDF) or, more informally, the Mass Democratic Movement. These diverse organizations formed a de facto internal ANC. Members followed the principles defined in the Freedom Charter (Document 18), calling themselves Charterists and often addressing each other as "comrade." Other fronts and organizations existed, especially those with a closer ideological affinity to the PAC and Black Consciousness—in particular, the Azanian People's Organisation (AZAPO). (Azania, an ancient Mediterranean name for southeastern Africa, was popular as an alternative name for South Africa by Black Consciousness followers.) They never commanded the support of the Charterist UDF.

The ANC struggled to keep up with this youthful internal rebellion. When the new generation's activists were imprisoned on Robben Island, Mandela and his cohort were taken aback by their defiance of prison wardens and regulations. Tensions also arose among those in exile. The liberation of Mozambique and Angola from Portuguese colonialism in 1975 led to new ways for the ANC to infiltrate South Africa (Document 24). However, even as the ANC in exile promoted a "popular war," they were ill-prepared to receive the defiant youth who fled the country to join the ANC's guerrilla war. Lack of discipline in the ANC camps, combined with the legitimate fear of enemy agents, contributed to violent practices. ANC soldiers tortured and sometimes executed insubordinate youngsters and alleged enemy agents, especially in the detention camps established by the ANC in Angola (Document 35).[5]

Within the country, the ANC tried to co-opt their rebellious comrades, sometimes by catering to the most violent elements. In 1986 Nelson Mandela's wife, Winnie Mandela, who provided the contact between the old ANC and the new resisters, declared, "With our boxes of matches and our necklaces we shall liberate this country," a reference to the practice of burning alleged enemy agents with gasoline-doused tires around them. A few young comrades formed ganglike organizations supported by arms smuggled in by MK cadres, as in the case of the Mandela United Football Club, more of an armed militia than a football (soccer) club. This group, which surrounded Winnie Mandela, terrorized the inhabitants of Soweto, punishing "sellouts" and on one occasion even murdering a fourteen-year-old alleged informer. Although examples such as these represent the excesses of the liberation movement, it was a time of fear and expectation, when violence held appeal and influence.

In the face of this rebellion, P. W. Botha (prime minister from 1978 to 1984, then president from 1984 to 1989; Document 31) sought to defend white South Africa from what he termed the "total onslaught" of communism. The Internal Security Act of 1982, a draconian ninety-nine-page law, permitted arbitrary detentions and suspension of habeas corpus. In 1985 a state of emergency all but suspended the rule of law. Branches of the security forces used "dirty tricks," including assassinations, espionage, spreading disinformation, and international anti-ANC propaganda, against the liberation movement (Document 32). The South African Defence Force (SADF) destabilized neighboring countries that offered ANC members refuge and allowed them to organize. In Angola, which bordered the northern part of Namibia, then occupied by South Africa, the SADF conducted brutal counterinsurgency operations against the ANC and its allies, in particular the South West Africa People's Organisation (SWAPO), which aimed at liberating Namibia from South African occupation (Document 34). Such operations certainly prolonged the Angolan civil war that had begun in 1975 due to rivalries between Angolan political movements. The end of South African intervention in the Angolan war began with the withdrawal from the Angolan town of Cuito Cuanavale in 1988 after sustained Cuban and Angolan efforts against the SADF. Although probably an exaggeration, the ANC viewed this as a decisive defeat for the apartheid army, which, the organization argued, led to South Africa's complete withdrawal from Angola, as well as from Namibia, and perhaps even contributed to the decision to seek a negotiated settlement within South Africa itself.

LIVING WITH APARTHEID: CLASS, RACE, AND GENDER

The majority of South Africans who lived during apartheid watched this dramatic political narrative from the sidelines. And yet South Africans were more than spectators. Apartheid was a part of their lives, even a way of life.

Regardless of the historical debate over whether segregation and apartheid benefitted capitalism, apartheid certainly inflated white incomes while keeping black wages low. Through the middle of the 1970s and then again in the early 1980s, the South African economy grew with buoyant gold prices. White families enjoyed unprecedented levels of wealth. The deep-level gold deposits, however, required cheap black labor to make them profitable. Black African men took these low-paying and dangerous jobs. They generally migrated to urban mining areas and left their families in rural homelands. Inequalities thus grew between rural and urban areas. Rural areas, hardly prosperous before apartheid, became impoverished, overpopulated, environmentally degraded, and largely unproductive except for cheap labor for the white-dominated economy. A poem by Mbuyiseni Oswald Mtshali poignantly evokes migrant workers' songs about their experiences in the gold mines and the effects of the separation of families (Document 39). The economic aspects of apartheid, which gave statutory force to the subordination of black labor, is the most distinguishing component of apartheid compared with other forms of racial and ethnic segregation, including Jim Crow laws in the United States, German Nazism, and Israeli Zionism.

Controlling the movements of blacks between city and countryside was an enduring aspect of apartheid. So-called influx control forced workers to leave their families behind in rural homelands. Africans (but not coloureds or Indians) had to carry a pass with them at all times in order to live in white urban areas. This pass became known as the *dompas*, or "dumb pass." The pass system left workers vulnerable. They dared not leave employers for fear that their right to remain in urban areas would be compromised. Without a pass, black South Africans could be imprisoned or deported to their homelands, and their families could be broken up. For fear of losing employment and the right to live in or near prosperous urban areas, vulnerable workers accepted these harsh conditions of employment.

Along with the pass laws, the most pervasive and intrusive aspect of apartheid was the forced removal of people to the Bantustan homelands. Between 1960 and 1982, some 3.5 million people (approximately 10 percent of the population) were forcibly removed. Apartheid authorities targeted those who lived on ancestral lands or who had sharecropped or even purchased land in white South Africa. Since rural communities were marginalized and poor, many removals went unnoticed by the outside world, even though they were resisted. There are scant documentary records of such removals and the gradual closing of livelihood options for rural black South Africans. The biography of the sharecropper Kas Maine, as told by the South African historian Charles van Onselen, is a remarkable exception.[6] An interview with a member of the Matoks community (Document 42) recounts how, through careful organizing in concert with the local chief, the community averted the forced removals suffered by their neighbors. Individuals on white farms, especially women, were defenseless against such policies, as demonstrated by the statement of a woman evicted off a farm (Document 45).

The Group Areas Act of 1950 targeted multiracial suburbs that existed close to the center of white cities. Forced removals in such urban areas were far more visible and led to organized forms of resistance. In the late 1950s, the destruction of Sophiatown, a suburb of Johannesburg, provided the testing ground for the ANC's first attempts to introduce mass resistance. They failed, and the white suburb of Triomf (triumph) was erected on its ruins. The predominantly coloured suburb of District Six, adjacent to the center of Cape Town, was known for its diversity and cultural vibrancy. During the 1970s, it, too, was destroyed, and its inhabitants were removed to the desolate Cape Flats, several miles from the city center (Document 41).

The chief challenge of apartheid policies was policing the boundaries between races, given white economic dependence on black labor. Pass laws and residential segregation managed to keep whites and blacks apart. However, many white families employed black servants within the domestic realm. Moreover, on the white-owned farms where many Afrikaners lived, black farmworkers and their families resided in close proximity to whites. The state tried to monitor interactions in this domestic realm (Document 37). The racial order required that white children disavow the early contacts they had with black servants and their children. Sometimes memories of such relationships could provide the basis for a nonracial consciousness, as was the case with the renowned anti-apartheid activist Bram Fischer (Document 38).

Apartheid laws contributed to gendered struggles. South African scholars have described how black women suffered a triple oppression: as workers, as blacks, and as women (Documents 28, 43, 44, and 45). Historians have also revealed the double-edged nature of changes in gender status during apartheid. When women managed to settle in urban areas, some were able to escape rural patriarchy and exert greater influence over their own households than they had in the countryside. In rare cases, such as the correspondence between the white liberal Mabel Palmer and the black orphan Lily Moya, female solidarity could emerge, although, as in this case, relationships usually remained paternalistic and never overcame the forces of race and class (Document 36). For vulnerable black women, education seemed the only way to escape marginalization, and they struggled, tenaciously but often unsuccessfully, to educate themselves and their children.

Apartheid also molded South African masculinities. White men affirmed their role as protectors of white women and of the apartheid order. Conscription into the army, restricted to white men, was an important part of male indoctrination (Documents 33 and 34). For black

South Africans, by cutting ties to families, migrant labor opportunities and the pass laws contributed to new black masculine identities. For many black and white men, closer connections developed between men regardless of race than between men and their families or between men and women of the same race.

The apartheid vision that black South Africans should remain rural subjects contributed to the unsettled nature of urban black townships. ("Township" is the South African term for separate black urban areas created by segregationist and apartheid policies.) As Jürgen Schaderberg's photos of Sophiatown reveal, black urban life could be vibrant, almost a renaissance, even as apartheid emerged. Sophiatown was bulldozed, however, and forced removals and influx control were traumatic and disruptive to urban life (Document 40). Political uprisings and school boycotts amplified the instability. With absent parents and domestic strife, youth congregated in gangs instead of homes and schools. The effects were contradictory: Youth were empowered *and* bore the brunt of violence. In practice, this contradiction was often (but not always) gendered, with young girls being the most vulnerable to sexual and other forms of violence (Document 44).

ENDING APARTHEID: REFORMS AND NEGOTIATIONS

By the 1980s, Botha's unyielding regime, matched by the uncompromising rhetoric of the liberation movement, made it seem that the end of apartheid would be achieved only through revolutionary violence. Although there was violence, the formal end of apartheid was less a revolution than a process of reform and negotiation that gave political rights to blacks but protected the economic privileges of the wealthiest whites.

In the 1980s, the vulnerability of the apartheid regime became apparent. Fluctuating commodity prices, worker disruptions, and international isolation threatened the economy. Internally, the rebellion had left vast parts of the country ungovernable. Botha realized the need for reform alongside repression. He tried to firm up separate development and co-opt Indian and coloured leaders (Document 46). This led to a new constitution that created a tricameral parliament, with different houses for whites, coloureds, and Indians. The liberation movement considered these reforms cosmetic, but the path to reforming apartheid had begun. Apartheid legislation began to be repealed, first the aspects of petty apartheid in 1985, and then the pass laws in 1986. Still, Botha continued political repression and rejected the liberation movement's demand for democracy within a unified South Africa. The end of the cold war and the fall of the Berlin Wall in 1989 pushed the reform agenda. The remaining international allies of apartheid South Africa—the United States and the United Kingdom—were no longer interested in supporting it as a bulwark against communism. After suffering a stroke in 1989, Botha resigned the presidency and was succeeded by F. W. de Klerk. In February 1990, President de Klerk lifted the ban on the liberation movements and promised to release political prisoners, including Nelson Mandela (but not yet all perpetrators of violence), opening the way for negotiations (Documents 47 and 48). The next four years were violent. In some parts of the country, there was a veritable civil war between ANC supporters and black opponents tied to ethnic patronage structures and egged on by the vestiges of the apartheid security apparatus. Chief among them was the Zulu nationalist Inkatha Freedom Party (IFP) of Gatsha Buthelezi. Fraught negotiations, especially over the drawing up of a constitution that would govern a post-apartheid South Africa, were frequently derailed, only to be put back on track by President de Klerk and Nelson Mandela. Both of these men went against members of their constituencies, formed a relationship, and tenaciously ensured the emergence of a post-apartheid South Africa. On April 27, 1994, South Africans voted in the first open elections. A united South Africa with nine provinces incorporating the Bantustan homelands came into existence (Map 3).

In addition to being a liberation of sorts, the end of apartheid was also a reining in of people's power, a counterrevolution even. The final reforms that led to the end of apartheid represented many compromises with established economic interests. Rights to property were protected; nationalization and economic redistribution were off the table. The 1990s were, after all, a decade of ascendant international neoliberalism. For many white South Africans, the end of apartheid carried no great cost. For many black South Africans, however, the ANC became an agent of whites and a few wealthy blacks, as Mondli Makhanya, then a young black journalist who would become the editor-in-chief of one of the most prominent South African weekly newspapers, feared when he cast his ballot for Mandela in 1994 (Document 49). Political freedom was exhilarating, but it meant much of the same for many black South Africans (Document 50).

One election could not end a massive project of social and political engineering that had institutionalized centuries-old prejudice in order to service a modern economy and entrench a racial aristocracy. Apartheid's legacies still shape South African lives. Inequalities, some of the

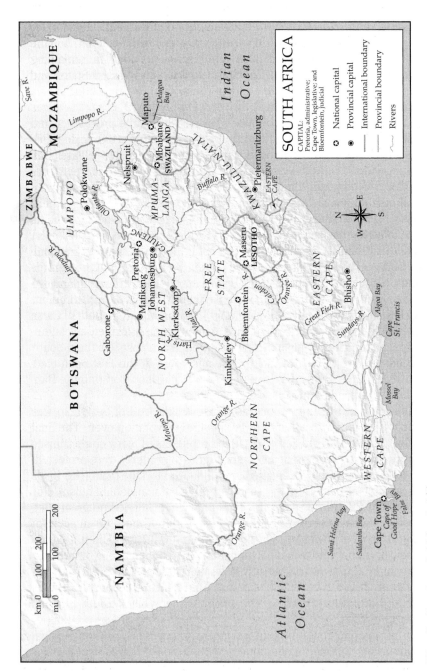

Map 3. *Post-Apartheid South Africa*

22

sharpest in the world, continue to fall along racial lines; poverty remains in rural areas, particularly in the former Bantustans; youth still struggle for education and opportunities; black workers labor under dangerous conditions and for low wages; and the unemployed and underemployed find little support from the state. These issues are recognizable in many poor and economically divided countries. Indeed, a reader of the documents that follow might detect that a global order that encourages the exploitation of cheap labor across guarded national borders resembles apartheid writ large. Was the end of apartheid more of a publicity stunt than a wide-sweeping change?

The history of apartheid told in this book is also the history of South African resistance to apartheid. This resistance has a legacy, too. For many South Africans, Nelson Mandela and his party, the ANC, became the symbols of the liberation that the people themselves had achieved. Senior ANC cadres were the immediate beneficiaries. The memory of iconic figures such as Nelson Mandela cuts both ways, however, just as it did when crowds booed South African and ANC president Jacob Zuma during the memorial service following Mandela's death in 2013. Apartheid has many legacies; the tradition of resistance, of people's power, forged in opposition to it should not be underestimated.

NOTES

[1]Stanley Trapido, "South Africa in a Comparative Study of Industrialization," *Journal of Development Studies* 7, no. 3 (1971): 309–20.

[2]In particular, the "liberals," who generally view racial attitudes as anticapitalist, versus the "Marxists," who argue for strong links between capitalism and segregation/apartheid. For an introduction to this complex debate, see Robert Ross, Ann Kelk Mager, and Bill Nasson, eds., introduction to *The Cambridge History of South Africa*, vol. 2, *1885–1994* (Cambridge: Cambridge University Press, 2011), 1–16.

[3]Saul Dubow, *Apartheid, 1948–1994* (Oxford: Oxford University Press, 2014), 113.

[4]Gay and Lesbian Archives, "Till the Time of Trial: The Prison Letters of Simon Nkoli" (GALA, University of Witwatersrand, n.d.), www.gala.co.za/resources/docs/Letters_of _Simon_Nkoli.pdf.

[5]For the Pango mutiny in MK and the ANC's defense of their actions, see "Further Submissions and Responses by the African National Congress to Questions Raised by the Commission for Truth and Reconciliation," May 12, 1997, www.justice.gov.za/trc/hrvtrans /submit/anc2.htm.

[6]Charles van Onselen, *The Seed Is Mine: The Life of Kas Maine, a South African Sharecropper, 1894–1985* (New York: Hill and Wang, 1997).

PART TWO

The Documents

1

Precursors

1

Natives Land Act

1913

The Natives Land Act of 1913 was the most significant law concerning indigenous Africans following the establishment of the Union of South Africa in 1910. By restricting black landownership and tenancy, the act laid the basis for long-term white control of 87 percent of South Africa's land.

1. (1) From and after the commencement of this Act, land outside the scheduled native areas shall . . . be subject to the following provisions: Except with the approval of the Governor-General—

> a) a native shall not enter into any agreement or transaction for the purchase, hire, or other acquisition from a person other than a native, of any such land or any right thereto, interest therein, or servitude thereover; and

> b) a person other than a native shall not enter into any agreement or transaction for the purchase, hire, or other acquisition from a native or any such land or right thereto, interest therein, or servitude thereover.

(2) From and after the commencement of this Act, no person other than a native shall purchase, hire or in any other manner whatever acquire land in a scheduled native area or enter into any agreement or

Union of South Africa, *Natives Land Act, Act No. 27 of 1913* (Pretoria: Government Printer, 1913).

transaction for the purchase, hire or other acquisition, direct or indirect, of any such land or of any right thereto or interest therein or servitude thereover, except with the approval of the Governor-General.

2

SOL T. PLAATJE

Cruel Operation of the Natives Land Act

1916

One of the founders of the South African Native National Congress (after 1923 the African National Congress, or ANC), Sol Plaatje recounts the effects of the Natives Land Act of 1913 on black Africans who held share-cropping arrangements with white farmers. Although Plaatje might have exaggerated the immediate impacts of the act, this remains a vivid description of the insecurities of life for rural South Africans.

We left Kimberley [for the Transvaal] by the early morning train during the first week of July, on a tour of observation regarding the operation of the Natives' Land Act. . . . We passed several farmhouses along the road, where all appeared pretty tranquil as we went along, until the evening which we spent in the open country, somewhere near the boundaries of the Hoopstad and Boshof districts; here a regular circus had gathered. By a "circus" we mean the meeting of groups of families, moving to every point of the compass, and all bivouacked at this point in the open country where we were passing. It was heartrending to listen to the tales of their cruel experiences derived from the rigour of the Natives' Land Act. Some of their cattle had perished on the journey, from poverty and lack of fodder, and the native owners ran a serious risk of imprisonment for travelling with dying stock. The experience of one of these evicted tenants is typical of the rest, and illustrates the case of several we met in other parts of the country.

Sol T. Plaatje, *Native Life in South Africa* (1916; repr., Braamfontein: Ravan Press, 2017), 78, 87–90.

Kgobadi, for instance, had received a message describing the eviction of his father-in-law in the Transvaal Province, without notice, because he had refused to place his stock, his family, and his person at the disposal of his former landlord, who now refuses to let him remain on his farm except on these conditions. The father-in-law asked that Kgobadi should try and secure a place for him in the much dreaded "Free" State as the Transvaal had suddenly become uninhabitable to natives who cannot become servants; but "greedy folk have long arms," and Kgobadi himself was proceeding with his family and his belongings in a wagon, to inform his people-in-law of his own eviction, without notice, in the "Free" State, for a similar reason to that which sent his father-in-law adrift. The Baas [Boss] had exacted from him the services of himself, his wife, and his oxen, for wages of 30s a month, whereas Kgobadi had been making over £100 a year, besides retaining the services of his wife and of his cattle for himself. When he refused the extortionate terms, the Baas retaliated with a Dutch note, dated the 30th day of June 1913, which ordered him to "betake himself from the farm of the undersigned, by sunset of the same day, failing which his stock would be seized and impounded, and himself handed over to the authorities for trespassing on the farm." . . .

Kgobadi's goats had been to kid when he trekked from his farm; but the kids, which in halcyon times represented the interest on his capital, were now one by one dying as fast as they were born and left by the road-side for the jackals and vultures to feast upon.

This visitation was not confined to Kgobadi's stock. Mrs Kgobadi carried a sick baby when the eviction took place, and she had to transfer her darling from the cottage to the jolting ox-wagon in which they left the farm. Two days out the little one began to sink as a result of privation and exposure on the road, and the night before we met them its little soul was released from its earthly bonds. The death of the child added a fresh perplexity to the stricken parents. They had no right or title to the farm-lands through which they trekked: they must keep to public roads—the only places in the country open to the outcasts if they are possessed of travelling permit. The deceased child had to be buried, but where, when, and how?

This young wandering family decided to dig a grave under the cover of darkness of that night, when no one was looking, and in that crude manner the dead child was interred—and interred amid fear and trembling, as well as the throbs of a torturing anguish, in a stolen grave, lest the proprietor of the spot, or any of his servants, should surprise them in the act. Even criminals dropping straight from the gallows have an undisputed claim to six feet of ground on which to rest their criminal remains, but under the cruel operation of the Natives' Land Act little children, whose only crime is that God did not make them white, are sometimes denied that right in their ancestral home.

3

SOUTH AFRICAN NATIVE NATIONAL CONGRESS

Resolution against the Natives Land Act
1916

The first political statement of the South African Native National Congress argues against the hypocrisy and white self-interest of the Natives Land Act of 1913, even while it is not explicitly against territorial segregation. As a strategy, the resolution calls for lobbying imperial political institutions, but it does not yet envisage mass political mobilization.

Having heard the main features of the Report of the Natives Land Commission on the Natives Land Act of 1913, and having learnt its principal recommendations, this meeting of the South African Native National Congress held at Pietermaritzburg, Natal, this 2nd day of October 1916, resolves:—

1.

That looking to the interests and welfare of the Bantu people within the Union, the Report of the Natives Land Commission as presented to Parliament is disappointing and unsatisfactory, and fails to carry out the alleged principle of territorial separation of the races on an equitable basis for the following reasons:—

South African Native National Congress, "Resolution against the Natives Land Act 1913 and the Report of the Natives Land Commission, 1916," in *From Protest to Challenge: A Documentary History of African Politics in South Africa, 1882–1964*, ed. Thomas Karis and Gwendolyn M. Carter, vol. 1, *Protest and Hope, 1882–1934*, by Sheridan Johns III (Stanford, Calif.: Hoover Institution, 1972), 86, 88.

That it confirms all our previous apprehensions prior to the passing of the Act: That it offers no alternative for the restriction of the free right to acquire land or interest in land: It recommends no practical or equitable remedy for the removal of the manifold objectionable disabilities imposed on the Natives by the Natives Land Act.

That it has failed to fulfill the official promises made to the Natives and also to satisfy their anticipations that the Report of the Commission would provide more land sufficient for occupation for themselves and their stock.

Whereas the land now demarcated or recommended by the Commission is inadequate for permanent settlement or occupation in proportion to the needs of the present and future Native population: And Whereas the said land is, in most parts, unsuitable for human habitation as also for agricultural or pastoral requirements, seeing that it has been studiously selected on the barren, marshy and malarial districts more especially in the Provinces of the Transvaal and the Orange Free State:

And whereas according to the evidence given before the Commission there is conflict of opinion amongst the whites as to the approval or disapproval of the principle of the Natives Land Act—the majority of the whites in the Northern Provinces are opposed to the Natives having the right to purchase land or acquire any interest in land in their own names: Nor are they in favour of any large tracts of land being granted to Natives for occupation or settlement except in the unsuitable districts as aforesaid.

By reason of these facts the Report of the Commission as presented for consideration by Parliament cannot be acceptable as a basis for the alleged intended territorial separation of the races or as a fair application of the alleged principles of the Act, on just and equitable lines. . . .

In spite of our previous promises to desist from agitation in connection with the Natives Land Act 1913, and recognising the Act is still in operation with detrimental effects to our people, the Executive Committee is instructed to immediately inaugurate a campaign for the collection of funds for the purposes of this resolution and to educate the Bantu people by directing their attention towards this iniquitous law.

That this resolution be sent to the Governor-General, the Missionary Societies and other interested bodies, and to the Anti-Slavery and Aborigines Protection Society. That the Chief Executive appoint a deputation of three to place this resolution before the Union Government at the earliest opportunity and also to lay same before the Union Parliament next session.

4

JAN C. SMUTS

The Racial and Moral Axioms

1917

Friend and foe of the British Empire, and signatory to the founding of the League of Nations and the United Nations, Cambridge-educated Jan Christiaan Smuts served as prime minister of South Africa from 1919 to 1924 and 1939 to 1948. Smuts was by white South African standards a moderate Afrikaner who brought Boer and Brit together, united by their differences from black South Africans. For Smuts, segregation was a salutary vehicle for racial unity and civilization.

Our problem of white racial unity is being solved in the midst of the black environment in South Africa. . . . We have started by creating a new white base in South Africa and today we are in a position to move forward towards the North and the civilisation of the African Continent. Our problem is a very difficult one, however; quite unique in its way. In the United States there is a similar problem of black and white with the negro population. But there you have had an overwhelming white population with a smaller negro element in the midst of it. In South Africa the situation is reversed. There you have an overwhelming black population with a small white population which has got a footing there and which has been trying to make that footing secure for more than two centuries.

You will therefore understand that a problem like that is not only uncertain in its ultimate prospects, but is most difficult in the manner that it should be dealt with. Much experience has been gained, and there are indications that we have come to some certain results. You remember how some Christian missionaries, who went to South Africa in the first half of the nineteenth century in their full belief in human brotherhood, proceeded to marry native wives to prove the faith that was in them. We have gained sufficient experience since then to smile at that point of view. With us there are certain axioms now in regard to the relations of white

Jan C. Smuts, "The Future of South and Central Africa," in *War-Time Speeches: A Compilation of Public Utterances in Great Britain* (New York: George H. Doran, 1917), 76–81.

and black; and the principal one is "no intermixture of blood between the two colours." It is probably true that earlier civilisations have largely failed because that principle was never recognised, civilising races being rapidly submerged in the quicksands of the African blood. It has now become an accepted axiom in our dealings with the natives that it is dishonourable to mix white and black blood.

We have settled another axiom, and that is that in all our dealings with the natives we must build our practice on what I believe Lord Cromer has called the granite bedrock of the Christian moral code. Honesty, fair-play, justice, and the ordinary Christian virtues must be the basis of all our relations with the natives. We don't always practise them. We don't always practise that exalted doctrine, but the vast bulk of the white population in South Africa believe sincerely in that doctrine as correct and true; they are convinced that they must stick to the fundamental Christian morality if they want to do their duty to the natives and make a success of their great country. . . . Natives have the simplest minds, understand only the simplest ideas or ideals, and are almost animal-like in the simplicity of their minds and ways. If we want to make a success of our native policy in South Africa we shall have to proceed on the simplest moral lines and on that basis of the Christian moral code. I think we are all agreed on those two points—on what I have called the racial and moral axioms. . . .

We have felt more and more that if we are to solve our native question it is useless to try to govern black and white in the same system, to subject them to the same institutions of government and legislation. They are different not only in colour but in minds and in political capacity, and their political institutions should be different, while always proceeding on the basis of self-government. . . .We have now legislation before the Parliament of the Union in which an attempt is made to put into shape these ideas I am talking of, and to create all over South Africa, wherever there are any considerable native communities, independent self-governing institutions for them. Instead of mixing up black and white in the old haphazard way, which instead of lifting up the black degraded the white, we are now trying to lay down a policy of keeping them apart as much as possible in our institutions. In land ownership settlement and forms of government we are trying to keep them apart, and in that way laying down in outline a general policy which it may take a hundred years to work out, but which in the end may be the solution of our native problem. . . . The natives will, of course, be free to go and to work in the white areas, but as far as possible the administration of white and black areas will be separated, and such that each will be satisfied and developed according to its own proper lines.

5

GERHARDUS ELOFF

Segregation with Guardianship
1942

*As a lecturer at the University of Witwatersrand and as head of the Depart-
ment of Genetics at the University of the Orange Free State, Gerhardus
Eloff advocated for the study of racial traits and insisted on the superiority of the white race in particular and racial purity in general. In the
concluding section of his book* Rasse en rassevermenging *(Races and
Race Mixing), he argues for the scientific basis for racial segregation and
the maintenance of white supremacy, or "status differences," as he puts it.*

The severity of the problem of racial interbreeding is scientifically based.
Miscegenation between whites and natives contradicts racial hygiene in
South Africa. Yet we find a rising negative attitude toward this view. This
is due to the dissemination of communist ideas. For the communist, the
emphasis on racial differences strikes against camaraderie between people
of different races. For a world paradise, the making of human brotherhood is required, and therefore miscegenation is desirable. For these
idealists, environment is the main cause of racial differences—and the
genetic and racial traits that the hereditary differences between races
and people demonstrate, without however ignoring the environmental
impacts that undoubtedly still exist, are wicked. Thus Russia wrecked
a large genetic congress. For world peace, world homogeneity is desirable, claims the communist. Interbreeding would assist in this. Do away
with status differences between white and black or coloured as it forms
a major bulwark against interbreeding. Fortunately enough, this communist racial conception has not gained ground with the Boer nation
[*volk*].

But we advocate racial purity for the other parts of our white population and with gratitude have noted that many of these whites also tend

---

Gerhardus Eloff, *Rasse en rassevermenging: Die boerevolk gesien van die standpunt van
die rasseleer* (Bloemfontein: Nasionale Pers, 1942), 101–4. Translated by the editor.

to the traditional view of the Boer. Thereby the Boer tradition [of racial purity] is saving other white people. . . .

In order that scientific grounds are established to hold up our Boer tradition of maintaining status differences and the dislike of miscegenation, it is necessary that genetic and racial studies gain a recognized place in our schools and universities. Further, it is necessary that a thorough survey and racial scientific study is made of our people, especially the Boer nation.

Maintaining the pure race tradition of the Boer nation must at all costs and in all effective ways be protected as a sacred pledge entrusted to us by our ancestors as part of God's plan for our nation. Any movement, school, or individual who acts against this should be treated as a racial criminal by the government and effectively dealt with.

In contrast, the Native and Coloured must be treated—according to our Christian beliefs as passed down by our ancestors—as less endowed, but nevertheless as creatures of God. The guardianship must be one that can withstand the toughest test.

6

SAUER COMMISSION

Apartheid

1947

In 1947 the Herenigde (Reunited) National Party (later the NP) of D. F. Malan, which would win the general election the following year, established a commission on the "colour question" headed by P. O. Sauer, a Nationalist member of parliament. The commission's report formed the basis for the NP campaign platform in the 1948 elections. In this abridged version, a translation of the unpublished report submitted to the NP, the basic policies of apartheid, and the justification for these policies, are outlined with regard to the three "non-white" races: "Natives," coloureds, and Indians. Laws would follow these vague principles over the next three decades.

Introduction

We have, in terms of policy toward the non-white races, two directions in South Africa. On the one hand there is the policy of apartheid, and on the other we have the policy of equality.

EQUALITY

The policy of equality has two schools of thought. One school, communist oriented, denies the fundamental nature of the existing differences

Verslag van die Kleurvraagstuk-Kommissie van die Herenigde Nasionale Party (1947), 1–5, 7–8, 16. Abridged and translated by the editor.

between white and non-white and therefore proposes, deliberately and openly, the establishment of mixed people in South Africa, where the colour bar will be wholly done away with. The other school of thought is not exactly in favor of miscegenation and does not propose open social equality, but refuses to take real steps against racial mixing and advocates equal rights and opportunities for all developed people, regardless of race or colour, within the same state structure. As the non-white races prove that they are qualified to use their democratic right, the whites gradually give them voting rights. They are in favor of the eventual removal of all color barriers in our national life. Approached with sober realism it is clear that both of these schools of thought lead to eventual assimilation. The only difference is the way and the time taken to achieve it.

The policy of equality or any variant of it must necessarily lead to the undermining and eventual destruction of the white race as an independent and governing people. This is the logical consequence of the numerical superiority and rapid development of the non-white races. Any speculation on the matter is wishful thinking and an illusion.

APARTHEID

The policy of apartheid has grown from the experience of the established white population of the country, Afrikaans and English speakers. It is based on the Christian principles of justice and fairness and the belief that the separate development of the white and non-white national groups [*volksdele*] in parts of our country is the only basis on which all national groups can truly be treated with justice and fairness, and each given a full chance to maintain and develop their own particular national nature and character. Any form of suppression is rejected as wrong, harmful for both white and non-white nations, and contrary to the policy of apartheid.

The principal aims of the policy of apartheid are:—

1. Maintaining the white population of South Africa as a pure white race through the complete elimination of any miscegenation between white and non-white, its consolidation as an independent political community, and its further development on a Christian national basis through the protection in all fields of a clear dividing line between white and non-white, and thereby the elimination of all possible sources of clash of interest between white and non-white.

2. Maintaining the indigenous non-white racial groups in South Africa as separate national communities by combating all influences that undermine their respective identities, and establishing opportunities for them to develop apart, in a natural way, and in accordance with their own national

character and calling, brought to fruition by Christian civilization in self-subsisting national units.

3. Maintaining the traditional principles of guardianship. Cultivating national pride and self-respect by each group, and cultivating mutual esteem and respect between the different races and racial groups in the country. . . .

General Foundations

1. The Party accepts as the highest task and calling of the state the promotion of the prosperity of South Africa and the happiness and welfare of its people, white and non-white, and considers that this goal can best be ensured by the maintenance, protection, and perpetuation of the white race and white Christian civilization in South Africa. The Party accepts this as a fundamental basis of its policy and therefore undertakes to properly and effectively protect the white race against any policy, teaching, or onslaught that undermines its survival or places it in danger.

2. The Party rejects with firm determination any policy that leads to the equality and mixing of whites and non-whites, with the resulting loss of identity of these races.

3. At the same time the Party wants it recorded as its firm conviction that any policy of oppression and exploitation of non-whites by whites is inconsistent with the principle of civilization and the ethical and Christian foundation of our national life, and is entirely incompatible with its policy.

4. The Party holds the view that God desired there to be a variety of races and nations whose livelihoods and natural growth would be honored as a part of God's eternal plan. In South Africa God in His Divine Plan endowed the white race and non-white racial groups with profound racial characters and other differences. Each race and racial group has its own character, nature, calling, and destiny.

The Party believes that a definite policy of apartheid between the white race and non-white racial groups and the application of the apartheid principle regarding the non-white racial groups is the only basis on which the character and future of every race and racial group can be protected and made safe, allowing each race to be guided to develop in accordance with their own nature and calling, and thereby eliminating all possible sources of racial clashes.

5. Under the principle of traditional Christian Guardianship the Party accepts the task and responsibility to protect the non-white racial groups where necessary, and to develop them gradually, in natural and healthy

ways, materially and spiritually, according to their own people, nature, and calling, until eventually they manage their own affairs in independent and responsible ways.

6. In their own areas, the non-white racial groups will get full opportunity for development in every area, and will have their own institutions and social services developed, where the forces of the developed and progressive non-whites can be harnessed to their own national upliftment.

7. The ultimate ideal and goal for overall apartheid between whites and Natives, so far as practically possible, will be gradually implemented, always taking into account the country's needs and interests and with due care to disruption of the country's agriculture, industry, and general interests.

8. The land policy should be drafted and implemented in order to further the apartheid ideal in a healthy and natural way.

9. As far as possible apartheid must be forged between the different non-white ethnic groups and recognition given to the apartheid principle with respect to the ethnic groups of the Bantu.

10. A system of compulsory national registration for all sections of the population will be established. The current pass system will be replaced by a more reliable and less grievous identification system for Natives in white areas and whites in Native areas.

11. A permanent advisory body of experts regarding non-white issues will be brought into being, and a well-equipped ethnological institute will be established.

12. The State will exercise full supervision and guidance over the education and general upbringing of the non-white youth.

13. The Party wants to emphasize the fact that the racial issues of our country are domestic issues, which involve the happiness and welfare of our fatherland, and can be approached only with thorough knowledge and sympathy. Consequently, outside interference and destructive propaganda will not be tolerated.

14. The Party encourages the principle of consultation with interested governments and white groups in Africa and especially in Southern Africa for the purpose of trying to get uniformity on the big matters of principle in respect to the color question.

15. The Party holds the view that the color question is a national issue and therefore an issue that is in the highest common interests of all people of the country. Therefore it should aim to join all population groups that subscribe to the principle of apartheid and on this common ground gather all forces for the realization of the ideal of apartheid between white and non-white. . . .

Policy toward the Coloureds

THE PLACE OF THE COLOUREDS

1. The coloureds generally take a middle position between the whites and the Natives, and therefore the policy of apartheid between whites and coloureds and between coloureds and Natives must be maintained. The coloureds should be encouraged to appreciate their national identity and develop their national pride and self-esteem.

APARTHEID BETWEEN WHITES AND COLOUREDS

2. They must have separate living areas where they can be guided to manage their own affairs.

3. A policy of apartheid between whites and coloureds should be executed in social, residential, industrial, and political fields.

4. Special attention will be given to the execution of a policy of apartheid in our industry, workplaces, and transport system as far as it is practicable.

5. Mixed marriages between whites and coloureds should be banned, and interbreeding between whites and coloureds will be combated by all means.

APARTHEID BETWEEN COLOUREDS AND NATIVES

6. The principal policy of segregation between whites and coloureds will *mutatis mutandis* be made between coloureds and Natives.

7. The coloureds must be protected in areas where they are already established against invasion and unfair competition from Natives. . . .

Policy toward the Natives

GENERAL PRINCIPLES

1. The Native must be anchored in his nation. He must be guided and educated to appreciate and build his culture and national institutions. He will only gradually and where necessary be adapted to Western civilization. All immoral and nationally harmful elements in his culture and national institutions must be eliminated.

2. The Natives have to be led to build a separate national structure of their own, in which they can develop in all respects, with full opportunities for all individuals and all chances to bring to life their national ideals and aspirations in their own areas.

3. The policy seeks as far as possible to bring together the main ethnic groups and subgroups in their respective areas, where each one

can build their own central government system, and where they can be guided to develop as separate national units.

4. As far as practicably possible separate residential areas in the cities for coloureds, Indians and Natives must be designated.

5. In the Native areas Native interests must be decisive and in the white areas white interests. . . .

Policy toward the Indians

1. The Party holds the view that the Indians are a strange and alien element that cannot be assimilated. They can never be part of our country, and they therefore must be managed as an immigrant community.

2. The Party accepts as the basis of its policy the repatriation of as many Indians as possible, and suggests a thorough investigation into the feasibility of such a policy on a large scale. In view of the seriousness of the question, South Africa must be willing, if necessary, to make large financial sacrifices for the achievement of this goal.

3. No Indian immigrants will be allowed in the country.

4. As long as Indians are still in the country a definite policy of apartheid will be applied between whites and Indians in all fields as well as between Indians and other indigenous non-white groups as far as possible.

7

History Comes to Life in the Jan van Riebeeck Tercentenary Celebrations

April 4, 1952

A politically charged celebration of Jan van Riebeeck, the Dutch East India Company official who established a permanent outpost at the Cape in 1652, took place in 1952. Van Riebeeck's historical persona was resurrected that year as the father of white South Africa and the basis for white national unity. The celebrations culminated on April 6, the tercentenary of van Riebeeck's landing at the Cape in 1652, which during apartheid would be celebrated yearly as "Founders Day." Press reports on the

"History Comes to Life," *Cape Times*, April 4, 1952, 5.

historical pageantry in 1952 demonstrated the effort to unite English and Afrikaans speakers behind a common story of how this white nation was built over its three-hundred-year history—a story that ignored the indigenous majority.

Jan van Riebeeck, on his high statue at the Festival Stadium, looked down proudly yesterday morning as the pageant of South Africa's historical past moved round the arena in splendor and brilliance, richly dressed in rainbow colours, to the cheers of 30,000 enthralled spectators.

South Africa's first 300 years of history unfolded itself in just an hour—in which the crowd saw highlights and incidents they know only from history books, and applauded loudly for Boer heroes and leaders.

The grand pageant ended when the float representing the Festival's motto, "We Build a Nation"—in the form of two white horses rearing their forelegs to the sky, drawing a chariot, guided by a white-clad youth with a young girl holding the Union flag beside him—made the centerpiece of a beautiful tableau.

Round the arena were spaced mounted heralds—a fence of colour—and between them drummers and courtiers faced the stands.

As they stood, the choir sang tributes to the history in special songs until, led by the horsemen, the impressive tableau broke up and filed out of the Stadium.

As the pageant started, cheering rang out as the first float—Africa Dark and Unknown—followed blue-and-yellow-satin-dressed heralds and standard-bearers into the area.

While the floats wound slowly round the arena, the characters on them enacted the scenes they represented.

Francis Drake was knighted; Van Riebeeck's sailors sang; there were mutterings and murmurings against Willem Adriaan van der Stel; and when the huntsman blew his horn Lord Charles Somerset's dogs bayed obligingly. . . .

. . . And before the procession ended there were floats of Higher Education—with the torch of knowledge—and a float of Africa Awakes, with figures in white, symbolizing youth's strength and purity.

8

HENDRIK F. VERWOERD

The White Man's Domain in the World
May 31, 1966

In 1961 white South Africans declared a republic and left the British Commonwealth. In this speech, Prime Minister Hendrik F. Verwoerd, often termed the architect of apartheid, appeals to the spirit of republican nationalism among white South Africans. Verwoerd's speech was also directed toward the currents of world opinion, which advocated for decolonization, national self-determination, and African independence, along with the rejection of racism. He thereby tried to reconcile white supremacy with the spirit of African decolonization through the "separate development" of nations.

What then is this Republic of ours, the Republic of the builders of this new nation? I can say at the outset that this Republic is part of the White man's domain in the world.

When viewed in terms of space, the White man's domain in this world is fairly small: a tip of the great Asian-European Continent, Australia, New Zealand, great parts of the Americas, and this tip of the Continent of Africa which is the anchor too of Western civilization. The White man and all that he has created for humanity through the past ages, is of incalculable importance for civilization and for history, and not only for history that has passed. He, and the spirit with which he is endowed, the characteristics which led him to this day and will in the future provide his inspiration, will always be needed where order and peace and progress are desired.

But, while we see this Republic as part of the White man's domain, we are not unresponsive to the ideals of others. We see Africa, for example, as it is, a continent of many nations, each with its own degree of development, each with the form of government acceptable to itself, each with its own pace of progress—a continent of many nations, Black nations, and

Hendrik F. Verwoerd, "Speech on the Occasion of the First Quinquennial Celebration of the Republic of South Africa at Monument Hill, Pretoria, May 31, 1966," in *Verwoerd Speaks* (Johannesburg: APB, 1966), 724–27.

in the southern portion, White. If the world could only realize that this continent is no different from Europe with its many states and nations, and from Asia with its many states and nations! If it only could realize that in this Africa to which we belong, the differences are there and will remain there and must lead to the existence and co-existence of many widely different peoples and states. If only they could realize this, what great opportunities for better cooperation and better solution for all our problems we would then find! We are not insensitive to the ambitions of others. On the contrary we, who as a nation had to fight for what we have and who have achieved this freedom, cannot but understand similar ambitions in the breasts of others. Those who believe in their own nation and its separate existence are best capable of understanding the desires of others to achieve the same.

We understand the nationalism of each of the separate states of Africa. We understand the similar ambitions of the various nations and national groups at present within our own boundaries. And because of our own experience, we not only understand their ambitions, but would also wish to help lead them to fulfillment in the right way so that it can be an achievement not only for the selected few, a dictator or two, but for the masses, for their progress and their happiness.

This is a White republic, ruled by the White man, part of the White domain of the world, but with full understanding for the ambitions and the objectives of the Black man of Africa within our own midst, our closest neighbours and those farther afield. . . .

To the outside world we must also say that when the morality of our Republic is called in question, when it is said that we are not prepared to accept equality or assimilation with all who are in our midst, to them we must say that morality does not exist on the principle in which they believe, which they have experienced alone. Nations, various kinds of people who live close together, can solve that problem so easily called multi-racialism when there is multi-national existence. I question the morality of forced assimilation or absorption of peoples. It might be the way for some of the mighty nations of the world; it can be true that in the United States of America its huge majority of White people can assimilate, in the course of time, the non-Whites in their midst. If that is their policy, if that is their way of life, who are we to question it? It is their problem, it is their country, those are their peoples and it is their future which they must seek themselves in their own way. Perhaps that may be the best solution there and in the United Kingdom, which has created a similar problem for itself, it may also be the right way to absorb and to assimilate, but is it the right way for a country like the Republic of South Africa? If we were to apply that principle of assimilation as if it were the only moral solution for our problems, what would happen to the White man whose heritage this South Africa is, settled by his forefathers, built by them through three centuries and more, a home for its people, drenched with their sweat and the blood of these three centuries? Must the White population be assimilated and lost; must all that they possess and have gained be lost? Would this be right for them? Would this be right for the Coloured and the Indian minorities who would also have to be absorbed in spite of their differences, their own ambitions, partially their own religions? Must they be assimilated and lost? And for the Bantu, would it be right for them to become the dominating group, but in the course of that process to lose their various national identities and perhaps languages and customs and to suffer by being unable, as we know is the case, to direct and run and develop the degree of Western civilization this country has reached in the form of industrialization and more? Would this be right to their masses? The few who might attain power, may be satisfactory and may be wasters for all we know. The masses would become to a great extent unemployed and the land desolated, as we have seen elsewhere in Africa. Would it be just to them? Would it be moral to create the semblance of freedom, but in fact allow living conditions of slavery?

9

Apartheid Legislation
1948–1959

This selection contains excerpts of some of the most significant apartheid laws. The Population Registration Act (1950) legislated the recording of the racial identities of all South Africans. The Promotion of Bantu Self-Government Act of 1959 extended the Bantu Authorities Act (1951) to

Union of South Africa, *Population Registration Act, Act No. 30 of 1950* (Pretoria: Government Printer, 1950); Union of South Africa, *Promotion of Bantu Self-Government Act, Act No. 46 of 1959* (Pretoria: Government Printer, 1959); Union of South Africa, *Natives (Abolition of Passes and Co-ordination of Documents) Act, Act No. 67 of 1952* (Pretoria: Government Printer, 1952); Union of South Africa, *Prohibition of Mixed Marriages Act, Act No. 55 of 1949* (Pretoria: Government Printer, 1949); Union of South Africa, *Immorality Act, Act No. 5 of 1927* (Pretoria: Government Printer, 1927); Union of South Africa, *Immorality Amendment Act, Act No. 21 of 1950* (Pretoria: Government Printer, 1950); Union of South Africa, *Reservation of Separate Amenities Act, Act No. 49 of 1953* (Pretoria: Government Printer, 1953).

*make separate development into a full-fledged political system of indepen-
dence for Bantu homelands. African representation in the parliament was
thereby replaced by a "tribal" system of "Bantu" administration, an auto-
cratic form of indirect rule supervised by the white government through
the appointment of commissioner-generals for each "national unit." The
Natives (Abolition of Passes and Co-ordination of Documents) Act of 1952
controlled movement between these homelands and white South Africa. In
addition to these major features of apartheid, termed "grand apartheid,"
racial segregation in ordinary affairs, referred to as "petty apartheid,"
included the Prohibition of Mixed Marriages Act (1949), the Immorality
Act (1927), and the Reservation of Separate Amenities Act (1953). Not
included here are laws of political repression that gave sweeping powers to
the security forces, in particular the Internal Security Act of 1982, which
consolidated and expanded on the Suppression of Communism Act of 1950
and the Unlawful Organisations Act of 1960.*

Population Registration Act, 1950

. . . 5. (1) Every person whose name is included in the register shall
be classified by the Director as a white person, a coloured person or a
native as the case may be, and every coloured person and every native
whose name is so included shall be classified by the Director according
to the ethnic or other group to which he belongs. . . .

[6.] (2) There shall in respect of every native whose name is included
in the register, be included in the register the following particulars and
no other particulars whatsoever, namely—

(a) his full name, sex and the district in which he is ordinarily
resident;

(b) his citizenship or nationality, the ethnic or other group and the
tribe to which he belongs;

(c) the date, or if the date is not known, the year or reputed year,
and the place, or if the place is not known, the district of his
birth;

(d) his marital status;

(e) the year of his arrival in the Union, if not born in part of South
Africa included in the Union;

(f) a recent photograph of himself . . . ; and

(g) his identity number. . . .

19. (1) A person who in appearance obviously is a white person shall for the purposes of this Act be presumed to be a white person until the contrary is proved. . . .

Promotion of Bantu Self-Government Act, 1959

. . . Whereas the Bantu peoples of the Union of South Africa do not constitute a homogeneous people, but form separate national units on the basis of language and culture:

And whereas it is desirable for the welfare and progress of the said people to afford recognition to the various national units and to provide for their gradual development within their own areas to self-governing units on the basis of Bantu systems of government: . . .

2. (1) The Bantu population shall for the purpose of this Act consist of the following national units, namely

(a) the North-Sotho unit;

(b) the South-Sotho unit;

(c) the Swazi unit;

(d) the Tsonga unit;

(e) the Tswana unit;

(f) the Venda unit;

(g) the Xhosa unit; and

(h) the Zulu unit. . . .

3. A commissioner-general shall represent the Government with the national unit in respect of which he has been appointed. . . .

12. (1) A [Bantu] territorial authority—

(a) shall maintain the closest possible contact with the commissioner-general appointed for the national unit in question under the Bantu Self-Government Act, 1959;

(b) shall assume a leading role and where necessary afford assistance to tribal and regional authorities within its areas in connection with matters affecting the material, spiritual, moral and social welfare and the educational interests of the native population of that area;

(c) shall endeavour to ensure the effective development of justice and of courts of law within its area;

(d) shall have power at any time to convene a conference of the population within its area . . . ;

(e) shall be competent to advise and make representations to the Government in regard to all matters affecting the general interests of the Bantu tribes and communities in the area in respect of which it has been established or of the national unit . . . ;

(f) shall have power . . . to provide for—

   (i) the establishment of markets and pounds;

   (ii) the control of erection and maintenance of buildings;

   (iii) the licensing and allocation of trading and other sites in respect of natives; and

   (iv) any matter relating to the exercise of its powers . . . ; and

(g) shall have such powers, functions and duties . . . as may be assigned by the Governor-General. . . .

Natives (Abolition of Passes and Co-ordination of Documents) Act, 1952

. . . 2. (1) The Minister may . . . require every native of a class specified in the notice who has attained the age of sixteen years and is resident in an area defined therein, to appear before an officer during a period and at a time and place so specified, in order that a reference book in such form as the Minister may determine may be issued to such a native. . . .

3. (1) An officer before whom a native appears . . . shall . . .—

(a) in the prescribed manner take or cause to be taken the finger prints of that native and transmit such finger prints to the bureau; and

(b) issue to that native a reference book in which shall be recorded the appropriate prescribed particulars relating to such a native. . . .

5. (1) If at any time after the fixed date it is found that any native of a class specified in a notice . . . who has attained the age of sixteen years, is not in possession of a reference book, such native may be brought before a native commissioner or assistant native commissioner who shall . . .—

(a) take such native's finger prints for transmission to the bureau; and

(b) after such enquiries as he may deem necessary . . . issue to the native a reference book. . . .

(2) Any such native commissioner or assistant native commissioner may pending enquiries . . . make arrangements to ensure the appearance before him of that native on any subsequent date and may for that purpose, if he deems it necessary, cause the native to be detained in any reception depot, lock-up, policy cell or gaol, for a period not exceeding seven days, which period may from time to time be extended by the native commissioner or assistant native commissioner for further periods not exceeding seven days at a time: Provided that the total period of detention . . . shall not exceed thirty days. . . .

13. Any authorized officer may at any time call upon any native . . . who has attained the age of sixteen to produce to him a reference book issued to such native under this Act. . . .

Prohibition of Mixed Marriages Act, 1949

. . . 1. (1) As from the date of commencement of this Act a marriage between a European and a non-European may not be solemnized, and any such marriage, solemnized in contravention of the provisions of this section shall be void and of no effect. . . .

Immorality Act, 1927, and Immorality Amendment Act, 1950

. . . 1. Any European male who has illicit carnal intercourse with a native female, and any native male who has illicit carnal intercourse with a European female, in circumstances which do not amount to rape . . . shall be guilty of an offence and liable on conviction to imprisonment for a period not exceeding five years. . . .

2. Any native female who permits any European male to have illicit carnal intercourse with her and any European female who permits any native male to have illicit carnal intercourse with her shall be guilty of an offence and liable to conviction for a period not exceeding four years. . . .

3. Any person who procures any native female for the purpose of her having illicit carnal intercourse with any European male or who procures any European female for the purpose of having illicit carnal intercourse with any native male, or in any way assists in bringing about such intercourse shall be guilty of an offence and liable on conviction to imprisonment for a period not exceeding five years. . . .

Reservation of Separate Amenities Act, 1953

. . . 2. (1) Any person who is in charge of or has control of any public premises . . . may, whenever he deems it expedient and in such a manner or by such means as he may consider most convenient for the purpose of informing all persons concerned, set apart or reserve such premises or such vehicle or any portion of such premises or such vehicle or any counter, bench, seat or other amenity or contrivance in or on such a premises or vehicle for the exclusive use of persons belonging to a particular race or class.

10

ERNEST COLE

Apartheid Signage

1967

In 1967 Ernest Cole (1940–1990), a South African photographer exiled to the United States, published a series of photographs about South Africa titled House of Bondage. *The book revealed the multiple aspects of black suffering and resilience under apartheid. In these images, Cole reveals how the "infectious spread of apartheid into the smallest detail of living has made South Africa into a land of signs."*

11

GATSHA BUTHELEZI

The Zulu Nation and Separate Development
June 11, 1970

---

*Gatsha Buthelezi, the longtime and self-proclaimed leader of the Zulu
"nation"—in part through his leadership of the Zulu cultural and political organization Inkatha—used separate development to advance the
interests of the Zulu, which he perceived as his primary political constituency. At the same time, he offered mild rebukes of white prejudice and
the excesses of apartheid. This speech reveals his approach to separate
political development, the cornerstone of apartheid policy.*

It is my privilege to address you on this historic occasion in the History
of the Zulu people. The Zulu nation has been the last, but certainly not
the least to reach this milestone, which the other six ethnic groups have
already reached. The Zulu nation is for that matter the very last non-
white homogeneous group to enter this era of self-government within
the framework of Separate Development. All sorts of opprobrious terms
have been used to condemn the slow pace at which this has come about.
I think it would be well for us to remember the words of the British Pre-
mier Disraeli, at the time of the Great Zulu War. I refer here to the now
famous line quoted quite often, "A remarkable people the Zulu. They
defeat our Generals, they convert our Bishops, and put an end to a great
European dynasty." The Zulu are no less remarkable today than they
were when this memorable remark was made during the last century,
despite the vicissitudes they have gone through, throughout the years.
 This necessitates a brief historical survey which will put today's event
in its correct and proper perspective. Initially the Zulu people were
made to understand by officials of Your Department, Sir, that the Bantu

---

Gatsha Buthelezi, "Speech by Chief M. G. Buthelezi, at the Inauguration of the Zulu Ter-
ritorial Authority, Nongoma, June 11, 1970 (abridged)," in Thomas G. Karis and Gail M.
Gerhart, *From Protest to Challenge: A Documentary History of African Politics in South
Africa, 1882–1990*, vol. 5, *Nadir and Resurgence, 1964–1979* (Bloomington: Indiana
University Press, 1997), 669–70, 672–73.

Authority Act of 1951 was optional. It was for this reason that at a Conference of Chiefs convened by our late INGONYAMA [King] H. M. Cyprian Bhekuzulu ka Solomon to consider the Act, we decided that the matter be decided by the Zulu nation, who had to make the choice we were made to understand we had. As no steps were taken to implement our resolution, the matter rested there for a few years. Some tribes in Natal "accepted" the Act.

About 1967, officials of the Department of Bantu Administration told some of us that the Bantu Affairs Commissioners who gave us the impression that we had a choice in the matter "were wrongly instructed," that we were merely being consulted and that consultation did not mean we had to consent. Those of us who had been waiting for our people to decide had after this explanation no option but to comply with the law, as the question of "accepting" or rejecting the Act, fell away.

In spite of this directive from Pretoria, some tribes were still without tribal authorities, some had tribal authorities and some districts had Regional authorities and others still had no Regional Authorities. It was at this stage that our late Ingonyama saved the situation by having that important and historic interview with you, Sir, in August 1968. On that occasion he presented to you, Sir, a certain letter, the relevant extract from which is follows: "Sir, Your Excellency, I believe that with the establishment of a Territorial Authority, a new and historic day will dawn for the Zulu people. I believe this will be a step in the direction of giving my people the self-determination, self-government and eventual independence and freedom which is the natural ambition of every nation. . . ."

It is indeed very sad that our King was not spared to see with us today his dream for his people coming true. It was this historic visit of Ingonyama to Pretoria which has united his people, that is those who had "accepted" and those who after they were told they have no option, complied with the law. I remember him saying to me on the eve of his visit to Pretoria that whatever the merits or demerits of this law were, it was essential for us to have such a body as you have inaugurated so that we can speak with one voice. . . .

If what the Ingonyama asked for . . . materializes as we hope it will, it will be something quite unique in the history of the human race. It will be the first time (for) a Metropolitan power such as South Africa, to relinquish power voluntarily for a subject nation such as we are. South Africa itself struggled very hard to shake off the shackles of Colonialism. Other African countries have also struggled hard for their freedom. White South Africa, particularly the Afrikaners, value their freedom and independence so much, because they got these things through blood, sweat, and tears. If this can happen to us peacefully, then our late Ingonyama will rank as one of our greatest Zulu Kings. . . .

We wish also to plead with you, Sir, to see to it that your officials exercise more tolerance in applying influx control regulations for as long as the Zulu state is not yet a fait accompli, and as long as most of it is underdeveloped as it is today. . . .

We shall all rejoice if, when we eventually get our freedom, that this shall be freedom in the truest sense of that word. That is, freedom embodying all the four freedoms which were so well set out by President Roosevelt of America in 1941 when he said: "The first is freedom of speech and, the second is freedom of every person to worship God in his way, the third, the freedom from want and fourth is the freedom from fear." A South African Afrikaner leader added a fifth one, which is freedom from prejudice.

Thank you, Sir.

12

Meeting between Homeland Leaders and B. J. Vorster

January 22, 1975

This meeting was a consultative overture by Prime Minister B. J. (John) Vorster (r. 1966–1978) to the homeland leaders. It illustrates the thorny issue of black political rights outside the Bantustans and the limited autonomy of homeland leaders from white political authority. Those who voiced an opinion, such as Gatsha Buthelezi of KwaZulu and Kaiser Daliwonga Matanzima of Transkei, represented the most outspoken homeland leaders; many of the others in attendance remained silent.

"Transcript of Meeting between Prime Minister John Vorster and Homeland Chief Ministers, Cape Town, January 22, 1975 (abridged)," in Thomas G. Karis and Gail M. Gerhart, *From Protest to Challenge: A Documentary History of African Politics in South Africa, 1882–1990*, vol. 5, *Nadir and Resurgence, 1964–1979* (Bloomington: Indiana University Press, 1997), 646–51, 653.

THE HON. B. J. VORSTER: The Prime Minister said that he welcomed leaders in the New Year not only in their official capacities, but also in their personal capacities. He referred in particular to Dr. Phatudi [Chief Minister of Lebowa], who had been sick. He then suggested that business commences as time was short. . . .

THE HON. K. D. MATANZIMA: The Chief Minister of the Transkei thanked the Prime Minister on behalf of his Colleagues for words of welcome. He expressed gratitude that the Prime Minister had "summoned" him and his Colleagues, to have a discussion. He expressed a hope that the Agenda would be disposed of within a reasonable time.

THE HON. M. C. BOTHA: The Minister of Bantu Administration extended an invitation to the black leaders to go with him to the Mount Nelson Hotel,[1] for lunch at lunchtime.

The Prime Minister then called upon the Chief Minister to open the discussion. . . .

THE HON. K. D. MATANZIMA: The Chief Minister of the Transkei opened discussions in the following way: on the Security of Tenure and Home Ownership: . . . Sir, it is now about 52 years since the principal act was passed and by now South Africans of all races should be able to give judgment as to whether Blacks are mere sojourners or are a permanent population of the cities in which they live without allegiance to a Homeland. I submit that all reasonable men agree that blacks who occupy residential and business premises in the townships on a rental basis should now be regarded as a permanent part of the urban population until the contrary is proved. . . . What we ask is for freehold rights to property in townships occupied by blacks. . . .

THE HON. B. J. VORSTER: The Prime Minister made an observation to the effect that no white man can acquire land in freehold in the "Homelands." . . . He said the whole object of that provision was to prevent whites buying up all the black land. There can therefore be no change of policy on freehold [tenure]. . . . On the question of land ownership, it seems clear that there can be no change of policy, but some system of leasehold will be considered and the government would go into the matter and inform the Homelands Governments of the outcome of investigations in due course. . . .

---

[1] Under apartheid, Cape Town's most exclusive hotel.

Item (c) Influx Control Regulations:

THE HON. H. W. NTSANWISI: The Chief Minister [of Gazankulu] pointed out that the leaders had presented a detailed memorandum at the March 1974 conference. . . . He said that influx control regulations should be abolished, as they were a denial of fundamental human rights. They caused a disruption to African family life.

THE HON. B. J. VORSTER: The Prime Minister said that he hoped that the "homeland" leaders will appreciate that influx control regulations cannot be abolished altogether. This was a question of housing, of health and jobs. . . .

THE HON. K. D. MATANZIMA: The Chief Minister stated: "I think, sir, that people should be free to sell their labour to any part of the country."

THE HON. B. J. VORSTER: The Prime Minister posed a question that if there was no influx control and 50,000 blacks came to Cape Town, who would take charge of their housing and amenities.

THE HON. K. D. MATANZIMA: The Chief Minister posed the following question: "What about the case of a man from the Transkei whose wife is not allowed to visit her husband, who is employed?"

THE HON. T. N. H. JANSON: The Deputy Minister [of Bantu administration and Bantu education] said that certain rules were made, but they had to find out how they are applied to remove these pinpricks. . . .

THE HON. B. J. VORSTER: The Prime Minister said that this matter goes into the root of most of our problems. It was a practical matter. It was also a political problem, and he stated that we are all politicians. . . . A senior official, a certain Mr. Meyer, was making a report. He said that the black leaders had said that they, as politicians, were at the receiving end. The Prime Minister suggested that the black leaders should appoint three from their number to go with that matter with that official, to work out the hardships and see what we can cook out of it.

THE HON. M. G. BUTHELEZI: The Chief Executive Councillor [of KwaZulu] said that this is a sensitive political matter as the Prime Minister has said. These regulations apply only to Africans and to no other racial group. If he had his way as an African, these regulations should rather be scrapped. . . .

Item (e) Civil Rights for Blacks in Urban Areas:

The Prime Minister called upon the Chief Minister of Lebowa to lead discussions as set out in the agenda.

THE HON. C. N. PHATUDI: . . . It was indefensible to imagine that the people who live in these urban areas, should have a vote miles and miles away. After living in a place for three generations in the city, you cannot be interested in the country.

THE HON. B. J. VORSTER: "I want you to define what you mean by civic rights."

THE HON. C. N. PHATUDI: "This was a question of a man who lives in a particular community, he wants to have a right to own property."

THE HON. B. J. VORSTER: "We have already dealt with that."

THE HON. C. H. PHATUDI: The Chief Minister said that a way should be found whereby the urban African can participate in local government.

THE HON. K. D. MATANZIMA: The Chief Minister pointed out that the leaders wanted them to have local government.

THE HON. M. G. BUTHELEZI: "They must have a budget of their own."

THE HON. B. J. VORSTER: "Local Government?"

THE HON. K. D. MATANZIMA: "Local Government."

THE HON. B. J. VORSTER: "What is the position, Mr. Botha?"

THE HON. M. C. BOTHA: The Minister [of Bantu Education] stated that there was no provision for separate financial administration. . . . The City Councils did not want to delegate powers to these Urban Black Councils. . . .

THE HON. C. H. PHATUDI: The Chief Minister remarked to the effect the Urban Councils had no power at all.

THE HON. B. J. VORSTER: The Prime Minister wanted to know whether the leaders wanted the Urban Councils to be clothed with more responsibility. . . .

THE HON. M. G. BUTHELEZI: The Chief Executive Councillor of KwaZulu then proposed that the question of Soweto, as a Homeland, be looked into. He said there was no consensus amongst the leaders, and yet he felt it should be presented to the Prime Minister for what it was worth. . . .

THE HON. B. J. VORSTER: "As far as the proclamation of Soweto as a Homeland is concerned, it is out of the question." . . .

Item (g) Mass Removals of Blacks from Urban Areas:

THE HON. C. N. PHATUDI: The Chief Minister pointed out that these removals cause bitterness. He suggested that facilities should be provided. These people should not just be dumped. . . .

THE HON. M. C. BOTHA: The Minister objected to the use of the word "dumped" by Dr. Phatudi and said that the government took exception to the use of that word. He said that with due respect to Dr. Phatudi, he wanted to point out that compensation is provided to all. . . .

The Prime Minister suggested that Conference move to the next item, after the Chief Minister of Lebowa had indicated that he had nothing further to add. . . .

Item (k): The Detente in Southern Africa:

After distributing copies of the text of what he wanted to say to the Prime Minister, on the detente in Southern Africa, Chief Buthelezi read out the memorandum he had prepared, which reads as follows: *DETENTE IN SOUTHERN AFRICA* by M. G. Buthelezi:

We wish to repeat the felicitations we conveyed to the Honourable Prime Minister, by telegram, on the 15th of November 1974, concerning his initiatives in the present detente in Southern Africa. . . .

We were encouraged by the Prime Minister's assurances to us at our March Conference, when he said that he also does not believe in racial discrimination. Although the Prime Minister added that he believed only in differentiation, it was not, as it is not even now, clear to us what the difference is between discrimination and differentiation. . . .

THE HON. L. M. MANGOPE [CHIEF MINISTER OF BOPHUTHATSWANA]: "We would like to know the real import of these speeches, because there is an air of expectancy." . . .

THE HON. B. J. VORSTER: The Prime Minister said that in a way it was a pity that this important matter is raised so late, and that on account of the time factor, one cannot devote as much time as we should on this important matter. . . .

"As far as the political future is concerned, our policy is well-known. Each one of you stands on a platform created by this policy. A policy which does not give you entree only in South Africa, but a policy which also gives you entree in the world.

"It is my policy to make each and everyone of you independent to take your place at the United Nations, if you so wish." . . .

"With reference to what Chief Buthelezi has said: 'whether we can go back to our people and tell them that blacks are now going to share power and decision-making with their white countrymen in a new meaningful way.'" The Prime Minister asked what also had they done first around the table that morning. He found it strange that Chief Buthelezi now wants to share power and decision-making, as he had refused it, when this was offered to him that morning. . . . The Prime Minister went on to say that when it comes to political power, "[Y]ou gentlemen will have all your Countries. But when you are in my area, I will not share decision-making with you. You cannot have your cake and eat it." . . .

The Prime Minister then referred to Chief Buthelezi's memorandum on detente in Southern Africa, and the Prime Minister read out:

"I would like to make it crystal-clear that I am not saying these things in any spirit of ill-will or threats, but I feel that it is my moral duty, at this point in time, to point out, the only logical alternatives we have, if we do not want our people to resort to civil disobedience and disruption of services in this land. Not that I intend leading my people in this direction *at the moment*," (at this point the Prime Minister reiterated, "*[A]t the moment?*" and remarked[,] "[T]hat is noteworthy"). The Prime Minister went on to read: "—but I feel judging by the mood of my people, that it is timely, that I should point out if no meaningful change is forthcoming for them through the government's policies, this will come as a logical alternative."

After reading that portion of that paragraph, the Prime Minister said: "I don't want to consider this as a threat. I want to say that I have been threatened before, but I have never run away. There will be law and order and people will not be allowed to take the law into their hands. I thank you for this discussion." . . .

The Prime Minister said that he was not prepared to accept federation as a solution in these words: "I am not prepared to accept federation as a solution; I accept independent states. This is my frank opinion, if you do not accept it, then I am afraid there is nothing I can do."

3

Defiance: Creating a Liberation Movement

13

AFRICAN NATIONAL CONGRESS YOUTH LEAGUE

Manifesto

1948

Anton Lembede, Nelson Mandela, Walter Sisulu, and Oliver Tambo were the young firebrands of the ANC Youth League, founded in 1944. They rejected the tactics of the past and called for more confrontational protests against segregation and white supremacy. Their political rhetoric drew on African nationalism gaining currency after World War II.

1. Historical Basis of African Nationalism

More than 150 years ago, our fore-fathers were called upon to defend their fatherland against the foreign attacks of European Settlers. In spite of bravery and unparalleled heroism, they were forced to surrender to white domination. Two main factors contributed to their defeat. Firstly, the superior weapons of the white man, and secondly the fact that the Africans fought as isolated tribes, instead of pooling their resources and attacking as a united force.

"'Basic Policy of Congress Youth League.' Manifesto Issued by the National Executive Committee of the ANC Youth League, 1948," in *From Protest to Challenge: A Documentary History of African Politics in South Africa, 1882–1964*, ed. Thomas Karis and Gwendolyn M. Carter, vol. 2, *Hope and Challenge, 1935–1952*, by Thomas Karis (Stanford, Calif.: Hoover Institution, 1973), 326–29.

2. The Birth of the African National Congress

Thus the year 1912 saw the birth of an African National Congress. The emergence of the National Congress marked the end of the old era of isolated tribal resistance, and ushered in a new era of struggle on a national rather than on a tribal plane. The A.N.C. became the visible expression of [an] inner organisational plane. However imperfectly it did it, the A.N.C. was in fact an outward expression of the African people's desire for a National Liberation Movement, capable of directing their resistance to white domination and of ultimately winning the African's national freedom.

Yet from the very outset, the A.N.C. suffered from serious defects. The founders, great patriots no doubt, had no grasp of the concrete historical situation and its implications, and they were obsessed with imperialist forms of organisation. . . .

3. Recent Tendencies — Their Significance

Far reaching changes have taken place in the African National Congress within recent times. . . . Doubtless there is room for more drastic and revolutionary changes in the organisational form of Congress if this organisation is to live up to the people's expectations. As far as the matter and substance of Congress' outlook is concerned, the year 1944 saw a historic turning point, when the Congress Youth League came into life. From the very outset, the Congress Youth League set itself, inter alia, the historic task of imparting dynamic substance and matter to the organisational form of the A.N.C. This took the form of a forthright exposition of the National Liberatory outlook — African Nationalism — which the Youth League seeks to impose on the Mother Body. . . .

4. Basic Position of African Nationalism

The starting point of African Nationalism is the historical or even prehistorical position. Africa was, has been and still is the Blackman's Continent. The Europeans, who have carved up and divided Africa among themselves, dispossessed, by force of arms, the rightful owners of the land — the children of the soil. To-day they occupy large tracts of Africa. They have exploited and still are exploiting the labour power of Africans and natural resources of Africa, not for the benefit of the African Peoples but for the benefit of the dominant white race and other white people across the sea. Although conquered and subjugated, the Africans have not given up, and they will never give up their claim and title to Africa. The fact that their land has been taken and their rights whittled down, does not take away or remove their right to the land of their forefathers. They will suffer white oppression, and tolerate European domination, only as long as they have not got the material force to overthrow it. There is, however, a possibility of a compromise, by which the Africans could admit the Europeans to a share of the fruits of Africa, and this is inter alia:—

(a) That the Europeans completely abandon their domination of Africa.

(b) That they agree to an equitable and proportionate re-division of land.

(c) That they assist in establishing a free people's democracy in South Africa in particular and Africa in general.

It is known, however, that a dominant group does not voluntarily give up its privileged position. That is why the Congress Youth puts forward African Nationalism as the militant outlook of an oppressed people seeking a solid basis for waging a long, bitter, and unrelenting struggle for its national freedom. . . .

6. Forces in the Struggle for African Freedom

(a) *Africans:* They are the greatest single group in South Africa, and they are the key to the movement for democracy in Africa, not only because Africa is their only motherland, but also because by bringing the full force of their organised numbers to bear on the national struggle, they can alter the basic position of the fight for a democratic South Africa. The only driving force that can give the black masses the self-confidence and dynamism to make a successful struggle is the creed of African Nationalism, which is professed by the Congress Youth League of South Africa. The Congress Youth League holds that the Africans are nationally-oppressed, and that they can win their national freedom through a National Liberation Movement led by the Africans themselves.

(b) *Europeans:* The majority of Europeans share the spoils of white domination in this country. They have a vested interest in the exploitative caste society of South Africa. A few of them love Justice and condemn racial oppression, but their voice is negligible, and in the last analysis count[s] for nothing. In their struggle for freedom the Africans will be wasting their time and deflecting their forces if they look up to the Europeans either for inspiration or for help in their political struggle.

(c) *Indians:* Although, like the Africans, the Indians are oppressed as a group, they differ from the Africans in their historical and cultural background among other things. They have their mother-country, India, but thousands of them made South Africa and Africa their home. They, however, did not come as conquerors and exploiters, but as the exploited. As long as they do not undermine or impede our liberation struggle we should not regard them as intruders or enemies.

(d) *Coloureds:* Like the Indians they differ from the Africans, they are a distinct group, suffering group oppression. But their oppression differs in degree from that of the Africans. The Coloureds have no motherland to look up to, and but for historic accidents they might be nearer to the [Africans] than are the Indians, seeing they descend in part at least from the aboriginal Hottentots who with Africans and Bushmen are original children of Black Africa. Coloureds, like the Indians[,] will never win their national freedom unless they organise a Coloured People's National Organisation to lead in the struggle for the National Freedom of the Coloureds. The National Organisations of the Africans, Indians and Coloureds may co-operate on common issues.

7. South Africa: A Country of Nationalities

The above summary on racial groups supports our contention that South Africa is a country of four chief nationalities, three of which (the Europeans, Indians and Coloureds) are minorities, and three of which (the Africans, Coloureds and Indians) suffer national oppression. . . . We are not against the European as a human being—but we are totally and irrevocably opposed to white domination and to oppression.

14

People's Protest Day

April 6, 1952

The first manifestation of the assertive nationalism of the ANC Youth League (Document 13) was the launch of a mass ANC campaign against apartheid, termed the Defiance Campaign, on April 6, 1952, the same day the van Riebeeck tercentenary celebrations (Document 7) took place. The flyer excerpted here illustrates the rhetoric and demands of the new ANC commitment to popular acts of resistance.

April 6: People's Protest Day

The African National Congress has served notice on the Government that the Non-European people can no longer go on tolerating the ill-treatment they suffer in the land of their birth.

Today our people are suffering as never before under this Nationalist Government of Dr. Malan with its policy of Apartheid. Under high prices and low wages, we are starving, our cattle are being taken away. We are homeless—or if we have homes, "Group Areas"[1] threaten to drive us from them. Every day we are jailed and sent to farm-slavery for passes[2]—and now women and children are faced with the pass system too. We are insulted and bullied because of our colour. Under the Coloured Voters Act, the Anti-Communist Law, the Bantu Authorities Act, South Africa is being made a fascist state.

Forward to Freedom in 1952

This year 1952, marks three hundred years since, under Jan van Riebeeck, the first white people came to live in South Africa.

---

[1] The Group Areas Act of 1950, which segregated urban areas.
[2] Those found without passes could be jailed and subject to forced labor.

"'April 6: People's Protest Day,' Flyer Issued by the ANC (Transvaal) and the Transvaal Indian Congress," in *From Protest to Challenge: A Documentary History of African Politics in South Africa, 1882–1964*, ed. Thomas Karis and Gwendolyn M. Carter, vol. 2, *Hope and Challenge, 1935–1952*, by Thomas Karis (Stanford, Calif.: Hoover Institution, 1973), 482–84.

The Malan Government is using this occasion to celebrate everything in South African history that glorifies the conquest, enslavement and oppression of the Non-European people.

Nothing is said of the fact that South Africa has been built up on the sweat and blood of the working people. Nothing is said of the famous leaders of the Non-European peoples. Nor is anything said of the noble Europeans who fought for freedom for all.

This Van Riebeeck celebration cannot be a time for rejoicing for the Non-Europeans.

It Is Time to Put an End to Slavery in South Africa — Enough

That is why, now, the African National Congress, backed by the South African Indian Congress, Coloured Organisations and other patriotic leaders of the people have decided upon a mighty campaign of mass action against unjust laws and for democratic freedom. We demand the right to live as human beings. We want an end to all the laws that discriminate against us. We want the right to vote, to choose for ourselves who will make and administer the laws we live under. We demand Trade Union rights and freedom of organisation.

April 6, 1952

On Sunday, April 6, 1952, protest meetings and demonstrations will be held throughout South Africa as a first stage in the struggle for the Defiance of Unjust Laws, for the ending of oppression: the march to freedom.

THIS IS A CALL TO EVERY MAN AND WOMAN TO JOIN THE STRUGGLE FOR FREEDOM!

Come in hundreds of thousands to the meetings and demonstrations on April 6!

MAKE SOUTH AFRICA FREE

15

Demand for the Withdrawal of Passes for Women
1956

On August 9, 1956, the multiracial Federation of South African Women organized a march to the government building in Pretoria to protest the extension of apartheid's stringent pass laws to women. More than twenty thousand women delivered their demands, chanting a defiant warning to the apartheid government: "Wa thint' abafazi, wathint' imbokodo. Strijdom uzakufa." ("You strike the women, you strike a rock. Strijdom you will die.") In 1954 J. G. Strijdom, the hard-line Transvaal head of the National Party, had succeeded Malan as South African prime minister. In 1958 he would die in office, two years after the women's march. Despite the march, the pass laws were extended to black African women.

In March 1952, your Minister of Native Affairs denied in Parliament that a law would be introduced which would force African women to carry passes. But in 1956 your Government *is* attempting to force passes upon the African women, and we are here today to protest against this insult to all women. For us an insult to African women is an insult to all women.

We want to tell you what the pass would mean to an African woman, and we want you to know that whether you call it a reference book, an identity book, or by any other disguising name, to us it is a PASS. And it means just this:—

- That homes will be broken up when women are arrested under pass laws
- That children will be left uncared for, helpless, and mothers will be torn from their babies for failure to produce a pass
- That women and young girls will be exposed to humiliation and degradation at the hands of pass-searching policemen

"'The Demand of the Women of South Africa for the Withdrawal of Passes for Women and the Repeal of the Pass Laws,' Petition Presented to the Prime Minister, August 9, 1956," in *From Protest to Challenge: A Documentary History of African Politics in South Africa, 1882–1964*, ed. Thomas Karis and Gwendolyn M. Carter, vol. 3, *Challenge and Violence, 1953–1964*, by Thomas Karis and Gail M. Gerhart (Stanford, Calif.: Hoover Institution, 1977), 251.

- That women will lose their right to move freely from one place to another.

In the name of women of South Africa, we say to you, each one of us, African, European, Indian, Coloured, that we are opposed to the pass system.

We voters and voteless, call upon your Government not to issue passes to African women.

We shall not rest until ALL pass laws and forms of permits restricting our freedom have been abolished.

We shall not rest until we have won for our children their fundamental rights of freedom, justice, and security.

16

Nkosi Sikelel' iAfrika

ca. 1950s

Enoch Sontonga first composed "Nkosi Sikelel' iAfrika" (Lord Bless Africa) as a Xhosa spiritual in 1897. In the 1920s, the ANC adopted it as the organization's official anthem. At the same time, church choirs popularized the hymn across the urban areas around Johannesburg. In 1942 a Sesotho version emerged, with the first recordings of this version appearing in the 1950s. In popular performance, the Sesotho version was added as a second stanza to the original. By the 1960s, the hymn—its emotional plea invoking the struggle for freedom—became the single most dominant element of protest gatherings. In 1994 it became the first two stanzas of the new South African national anthem.

Nkosi sikelel' iAfrika
Maluphakanyisw' uphondo lwayo,
Yizwa imithandazo yethu,
Nkosi sikelela, thina lusapho
    lwayo. [isiXhosa]

Lord bless Africa
May her glory be lifted high,
Hear our petitions,
God bless us, Your children.

Several versions evolved from Sontonga's original. For a history of various audio recordings, see Siemon Allen, "The South African National Anthem: A History on Record," http://flatint.blogspot.com/2013/10/the-south-african-national-anthem.html.

Morena boloka setjhaba sa heso,	God we ask You to protect our
O fedise dintwa le matshwe-	nation,
nyeho,	Intervene and end all conflicts,
O se boloke, O se boloke	Protect us, protect our nation,
setjhaba sa heso,	
Setjhaba sa, South Afrika.	Our nation, South Africa.
[Sesotho]	

17

CONGRESS OF THE PEOPLE

Freedom Charter

June 25–26, 1955

Around three thousand individuals rallied for the Congress of the People held in June 1955 at Kliptown, in Soweto, to articulate their demands. They ratified the Freedom Charter, the content of which became the guiding principles for the ANC and its affiliates. Activists who adhered to the charter called themselves Charterists. For white authorities, the clauses regarding the sharing of the country's wealth proved that the charter was communist.

Preamble

We, the People of South Africa, declare for all our country and the world to know:—

That South Africa belongs to all who live in it, black and white, and that no government can justly claim authority unless it is based on the will of the people;

That our people have been robbed of their birthright to land, liberty and peace by a form of government founded on injustice and inequality;

That our country will never be prosperous or free until all our people live in brotherhood, enjoying equal rights and opportunities;

"'Freedom Charter,' Adopted by the Congress of the People, June 26, 1955," in *From Protest to Challenge: A Documentary History of African Politics in South Africa, 1882–1964*, ed. Thomas Karis and Gwendolyn M. Carter, vol. 3, *Challenge and Violence, 1953–1964*, by Thomas Karis and Gail M. Gerhart (Stanford, Calif.: Hoover Institution, 1977), 205–8.

That only a democratic state, based on the will of all the people can secure to all their birthright without distinction of colour, race, sex or belief;

And therefore, we, the people of South Africa, black and white, together—equals, countrymen and brothers—adopt this FREEDOM CHARTER. And we pledge ourselves to strive together, sparing nothing of our strength and courage, until the democratic changes here set out have been won.

The People Shall Govern!

Every man and woman shall have the right to vote for and to stand as a candidate for all bodies which make laws;

All the people shall be entitled to take part in the administration of the country;

The rights of the people shall be the same regardless of race, colour or sex;

All bodies of minority rule, advisory boards, councils and authorities shall be replaced by democratic organs of self-government.

All National Groups Shall Have Equal Rights!

There shall be equal status in the bodies of state, in the courts and in the schools for all national groups and races;

All national groups shall be protected by law against insults to their race and national pride;

All people shall have equal right to use their own language and to develop their own folk culture and customs;

The preaching and practice of national, race or colour discrimination and contempt shall be a punishable crime;

All apartheid laws and practices shall be set aside.

The People Shall Share in the Country's Wealth!

The national wealth of our country, the heritage of all South Africans, shall be restored to the people;

The mineral wealth beneath the soil, the banks and monopoly industry shall be transferred to the ownership of the people as a whole;

All other industries and trade shall be controlled to assist the well-being of the people;

All people shall have equal rights to trade where they choose, to manufacture and to enter all trades, crafts and professions.

The Land Shall Be Shared among Those Who Work It!

Restriction of land ownership on a racial basis shall be ended, and all the land re-divided amongst those who work it, to banish famine and land hunger;

The state shall help the peasants with implements, seed, tractors and dams to save the soil and assist the tillers;

Freedom of movement shall be guaranteed to all who work on the land;

All shall have the right to occupy land wherever they choose;

People shall not be robbed of their cattle, and forced labour and farm prisons shall be abolished.

All Shall Be Equal before the Law!

No one shall be imprisoned, deported or restricted without a fair trial;

No one shall be condemned by the order of any Government official;

The courts shall be representative of all the people;

Imprisonment shall be only for serious crimes against the people, and shall aim at re-education, not vengeance;

The police force and army shall be open to all on an equal basis and shall be the helpers and protectors of the people;

All laws which discriminate on grounds of race, colour or belief shall be repealed.

All Shall Enjoy Equal Human Rights!

The law shall guarantee to all their right to speak, to organise, to meet together, to publish, to preach, to worship and to educate their children;

The privacy of the house from police raids shall be protected by law;

All shall be free to travel without restriction from countryside to town, from province to province, and from South Africa abroad;

Pass laws, permits and all other laws restricting these freedoms shall be abolished.

There Shall Be Work and Security!

All who work shall be free to form trade unions, to elect their officers and to make wage agreements with their employers;

The state shall recognise the right and duty of all to work, and to draw full unemployment benefits;

Men and women of all races shall receive equal pay for equal work;

There shall be a forty-hour working week, a national minimum wage, paid annual leave, and sick leave for all workers, and maternity leave on full pay for all working mothers;

Miners, domestic workers, farm workers and civil servants shall have the same rights as all others who work;

Child labour, compound labour, the tot system [payment in alcohol] and contract labour shall be abolished.

The Doors of Learning and of Culture Shall Be Opened!

The government shall discover, develop and encourage national talent for the enhancement of our cultural life;

All the cultural treasures of mankind shall be open to all, by free exchange of books, ideas and contact with other lands;

The aim of education shall be to teach the youth to love their people and their culture, to honour human brotherhood, liberty and peace;

Education shall be free, compulsory, universal and equal for all children;

Higher education and technical training shall be opened to all by means of state allowances and scholarships awarded on the basis of merit;

Adult illiteracy shall be ended by a mass state education plan;

Teachers shall have all the rights of other citizens;

The colour bar in cultural life, in sport and in education shall be abolished.

There Shall Be Houses, Security and Comfort!

All people shall have the right to live where they choose, to be decently housed and to bring up their families in comfort and security;

Unused housing space to be made available to the people;

Rent and prices shall be lowered, food plentiful and no one shall go hungry;

A preventive health scheme shall be run by the state;

Free medical care and hospitalisation shall be provided for all, with special care for mothers and young children;

Slums shall be demolished, and new suburbs built where all have transport, roads, lighting, playing fields, crèches and social centres;

The aged, the orphans, the disabled and the sick shall be cared for by the state;

Rest, leisure and recreation shall be the right of all;

Fenced locations and ghettoes shall be abolished, and laws which break up families shall be repealed.

There Shall Be Peace and Friendship!

South Africa shall be a fully independent state, which respects the rights and sovereignty of all nations;

South Africa shall strive to maintain world peace and the settlement of all international disputes by negotiation—not war;

Peace and friendship amongst all our people shall be secured by upholding the equal rights, opportunities and status of all;

The people of the protectorates—Basutoland, Bechuanaland and Swaziland—shall be free to decide for themselves their own future;

The right of all the peoples of Africa to independence and self-government shall be recognised, and shall be the basis of close cooperation.

Let all who love their people and their country now say, as we say here: "THESE FREEDOMS WE WILL FIGHT FOR, SIDE BY SIDE, THROUGHOUT OUR LIVES, UNTIL WE HAVE WON OUR LIBERTY."

18

ROBERT M. SOBUKWE

Opening Address of the Pan Africanist Congress (PAC)

1959

Robert Sobukwe, the founder of the Pan Africanist Congress (PAC), rejected the Freedom Charter (Document 17), arguing that it was influenced by whites and paid insufficient attention to the spirit of African national-ism. Here Sobukwe describes the motivations behind the Africanist split

Robert M. Sobukwe, "Opening Address," in *From Protest to Challenge: A Documentary History of African Politics in South Africa, 1882–1964*, ed. Thomas Karis and Gwendolyn M. Carter, vol. 3, *Challenge and Violence, 1953–1964*, by Thomas Karis and Gail M. Gerhart (Stanford, Calif.: Hoover Institution, 1977), 514–16.

with the ANC and the creation of a rival liberation movement, the PAC.
The heady sentiments of African nationalism then spreading across the
continent are reflected in this speech.

The Africanists take the view that there is only one race to which we all
belong, and that is the human race. In our vocabulary therefore, the word
"race" as applied to man, has no plural form. We do, however, admit the
existence of observable physical differences between various groups of
people, but these differences are the result of a number of factors, chief
among which has been geographical isolation.

In Afrika the myth of race has been propounded and propagated by
the imperialists and colonialists from Europe, in order to facilitate and
justify their inhuman exploitation of the indigenous people of the land. It
is from this myth of race with its attendant claims of cultural superiority
that the doctrine of white supremacy stems. . . .

In South Africa we recognise the existence of national groups which
are the result of geographical origin within a certain area as well as a
shared historical experience of these groups. The Europeans are a foreign minority group which has exclusive control of political, economic,
social and military power. It is the dominant group. It is the exploiting group, responsible for the pernicious doctrine of White supremacy
which has resulted in the humiliation and degradation of the indigenous
African people. It is this group which has dispossessed the African people
of their land and with arrogant conceit has set itself up as the "guard-
ians," the "trustees" of the Africans. It is this group which conceives of
the African people as a child nation, composed of Boys and Girls, ranging
in age from 120 years to one day. It is this group which, after 300 years,
can still state with brazen effrontery that the Native, the Bantu, the Kaf-
fir is still backward and savage etc. But they still want to remain "guard-
ians," "trustees," and what have you, of the African people. In short it is
this group which has mismanaged affairs in South Africa just as their
kith and kin are mismanaging affairs in Europe. It is from this group
that the most rabid race baiters and agitators come. It is members of this
group who, whenever they meet in their Parliament, say things which
agitate the hearts of millions of peace-loving Africans. This is the group
which turns out thousands of experts on that new South African Sci-
ence—the Native mind.

Then there is the Indian foreign minority group. This group came to this
country not as imperialists or colonialists, but as indentured labourers. In
the South African set-up of today, this group is an oppressed minority. But

there are some members of this group, the merchant class in particular, who have become tainted with the virus of cultural supremacy and national arrogance. This class identifies itself by and large with the oppressor but, significantly, this is the group which provides the political leadership of the Indian people in South Africa. And all that the politics of this class have meant up to now is preservation and defence of the sectional interests of the Indian merchant class. The down-trodden, poor "stinking coolies" of Natal who, alone, as a result of the pressure of material conditions, can identify themselves with the indigenous African majority in the struggle to overthrow White supremacy, have not yet produced their leadership. We hope they will do so soon.

The Africans constitute the indigenous group and form the majority of the population. They are the most ruthlessly exploited and are subjected to humiliation, degradation and insult.

Now it is our contention that true democracy can be established in South Africa and on the continent as a whole, only when White supremacy has been destroyed. And the illiterate and semi-literate African masses constitute the key and centre and content of any struggle for true democracy in South Africa. And the African people can be organised only under the banner of African nationalism in an All-African Organisation where they will by themselves formulate policies and programmes and decide on the methods of struggle without interference from either so-called left-wing or right-wing groups of the minorities who arrogantly appropriate to themselves the right to plan and think for the Africans.

We wish to emphasise that the freedom of the African means the freedom of all in South Africa, the European included, because only the African can guarantee the establishment of a genuine democracy in which all men will be citizens of a common state and will live and be governed as individuals and not as distinctive sectional groups. . . .

We aim, politically, at government of the Africans by the Africans, for the Africans, with everybody who owes his only loyalty to Afrika and who is prepared to accept the democratic rule of an African majority being regarded as an African. We guarantee no minority rights, because we think in terms of individuals, not groups.

Economically we aim at the rapid extension of industrial development in order to alleviate pressure on the land, which is what progress means in terms of modern society. We stand committed to a policy guaranteeing the most equitable distribution of wealth.

Socially we aim at the full development of the human personality and a ruthless uprooting and outlawing of all forms or manifestations of the racial myth. To sum it up we stand for an Africanist Socialist Democracy.

Here is a tree rooted in African soil, nourished with waters from the rivers of Afrika. Come and sit under its shade and become, with us, the leaves of the same branch and the branches of the same tree.

Sons and Daughters of Afrika, I declare this inaugural convention of the Africanists open! IZWE LETHU!! [Our Nation!!]

19

ALBERT JOHN MVUMBI LUTULI

Nobel Lecture

December 11, 1961

Albert John Mvumbi Lutuli (also known as Chief Albert Luthuli) was the Nobel Peace Prize laureate in 1961. He was a chief in Groutville, Natal, before being dismissed from the chieftainship in 1952 by the government due to his support for the ANC's Defiance Campaign (see Document 14). Educated at a Methodist mission, Lutuli based his ideas on Christian morality and advocated for Christian passive resistance. Although he was a Zulu chief, Lutuli's nationalism went beyond apartheid-inspired tribal units and instead mobilized behind an inclusive pan-Africanism. Lutuli remained head of the ANC following its banning in 1960 and stayed in that position until 1967. Even as he advocated for nonviolent resistance in his Nobel Lecture, his stance was increasingly marginalized within the ANC, where Nelson Mandela and others had begun planning for an armed struggle. In 1967, Lutuli died after being struck by a train.

Africa and Freedom

In years gone by, some of the greatest men of our century have stood here to receive this award, men whose names and deeds have enriched the pages of human history, men whom future generations will regard as having shaped the world of our time. No one could be left unmoved at being plucked from the village of Groutville, a name many of you have

---

Albert Lutuli, "Nobel Lecture," December 11, 1961, www.nobelprize.org/nobel_prizes /peace/laureates/1960/lutuli-lecture.html.

never heard before and which does not even feature on many maps—to be plucked from banishment in a rural backwater, to be lifted out of the narrow confines of South Africa's internal politics and placed here in the shadow of these great figures. It is a great honor to me to stand on this rostrum where many of the great men of our times have stood before.

The Nobel Peace Award that has brought me here has for me a three-fold significance. On the one hand, it is a tribute to my humble contribution to efforts by democrats on both sides of the color line to find a peaceful solution to the race problem. This contribution is not in any way unique. I did not initiate the struggle to extend the area of human freedom in South Africa; other African patriots—devoted men—did so before me. I also, as a Christian and patriot, could not look on while systematic attempts were made, almost in every department of life, to debase the God-factor in man or to set a limit beyond which the human being in his black form might not strive to serve his Creator to the best of his ability. To remain neutral in a situation where the laws of the land virtually criticized God for having created men of color was the sort of thing I could not, as a Christian, tolerate.

On the other hand, the award is a democratic declaration of solidarity with those who fight to widen the area of liberty in my part of the world. As such, it is the sort of gesture which gives me, and millions who think as I do, tremendous encouragement. There are still people in the world today who regard South Africa's race problem as a simple clash between black and white. Our government has carefully projected this image of the problem before the eyes of the world. This has had two effects. It has confused the real issues at stake in the race crisis. It has given some form of force to the government's contention that the race problem is a domestic matter for South Africa. This, in turn, has tended to narrow down the area over which our case could be better understood in the world.

From yet another angle, it is welcome recognition of the role played by the African people during the last fifty years to establish, peacefully, a society in which merit and not race would fix the position of the individual in the life of the nation.

This award could not be for me alone, nor for just South Africa, but for Africa as a whole. Africa presently is most deeply torn with strife and most bitterly stricken with racial conflict. How strange then it is that a man of Africa should be here to receive an award given for service to the cause of peace and brotherhood between men. There has been little peace in Africa in our time. From the northernmost end of our continent, where war has raged for seven years, to the center and to the south there are battles being fought out, some with arms, some without. In my own country, in the year 1960, for which this award is given, there was a state of emergency for many months. At Sharpeville, a small village, in a single afternoon sixty-nine people were shot dead and 180 wounded by small arms fire; and in parts like the Transkei, a state of emergency is still continuing. Ours is a continent in revolution against oppression. And peace and revolution make uneasy bedfellows. There can be no peace until the forces of oppression are overthrown.

Our continent has been carved up by the great powers; alien governments have been forced upon the African people by military conquest and by economic domination; strivings for nationhood and national dignity have been beaten down by force; traditional economics and ancient customs have been disrupted, and human skills and energy have been harnessed for the advantage of our conquerors. In these times there has been no peace; there could be no brotherhood between men. . . .

There is a paradox in the fact that Africa qualifies for such an award in its age of turmoil and revolution. How great is the paradox and how much greater the honor that an award in support of peace and the brotherhood of man should come to one who is a citizen of a country where the brotherhood of man is an illegal doctrine, outlawed, banned, censured, proscribed and prohibited; where to work, talk, or campaign for the realization in fact and deed of the brotherhood of man is hazardous, punished with banishment, or confinement without trial, or imprisonment; where effective democratic channels to peaceful settlement of the race problem have never existed these 300 years; and where white minority power rests on the most heavily armed and equipped military machine in Africa. This is South Africa.

Even here, where white rule seems determined not to change its mind for the better, the spirit of Africa's militant struggle for liberty, equality, and independence asserts itself. I, together with thousands of my countrymen, have in the course of the struggle for these ideals been harassed and imprisoned, but we are not deterred in our quest for a new age in which we shall live in peace and in brotherhood.

It is not necessary for me to speak at length about South Africa; its social system, its politics, its economics, and its laws have forced themselves on the attention of the world. It is a museum piece in our time, a hangover from the dark past of mankind, a relic of an age which everywhere else is dead or dying. Here the cult of race superiority and of white supremacy is worshiped like a god. Few white people escape corruption, and many of their children learn to believe that white men are unquestionably superior, efficient, clever, industrious, and capable; that black men are, equally unquestionably, inferior, slothful, stupid, evil, and clumsy. On the basis of the mythology that "the lowest amongst them is higher than the highest amongst us," it is claimed that white men build everything that is worthwhile in the country—its cities, its industries, its mines, and its agriculture and that they alone are thus fitted and entitled as of right to own and control these things, while black men are only temporary sojourners in these cities, fitted only for menial labor, and unfit to share political power. The prime minister of South Africa, Dr. Verwoerd, then minister of Bantu Affairs, when explaining his government's policy on African education had this to say: "There is no place for him (the African) in the European community above the level of certain forms of labor."

There is little new in this mythology. Every part of Africa which has been subject to white conquest has, at one time or another and in one guise or another, suffered from it, even in its virulent form of the slavery that obtained in Africa up to the nineteenth century. The mitigating feature in the gloom of those far-off days was the shaft of light sunk by Christian missions, a shaft of light to which we owe our initial enlightenment. With successive governments of the time doing little or nothing to ameliorate the harrowing suffering of the black man at the hands of slave drivers, men like Dr. David Livingstone and Dr. John Philip and other illustrious men of God stood for social justice in the face of overwhelming odds. It is worth noting that the names I have referred to are still anathema to some South Africans. Hence the ghost of slavery lingers on to this day in the form of forced labor that goes on in what are called farm prisons. But the tradition of Livingstone and Philip lives on, perpetuated by a few of their line. It is fair to say that even in present-day conditions, Christian missions have been in the vanguard of initiating social services provided for us. Our progress in this field has been in spite of, and not mainly because of, the government. In this, the church in South Africa, though belatedly, seems to be awakening to a broader mission of the church in its ministry among us. It is beginning to take seriously the words of its Founder who said: "I came that they might have life and have it more abundantly." This is a call to the church in South Africa to help in the all-round development of man in the present, and not only in the hereafter. In this regard, the people of South Africa, especially those who claim to be Christians, would be well advised to take heed of the Conference decisions of the World Council of Churches held at Cottesloe, Johannesburg, in 1960, which gave a clear lead on the mission of the church in our day. It left no room for doubt about the relevancy of the Christian message in the present issues that confront mankind. I note with gratitude this broader outlook of the World Council of Churches. It has a great meaning and significance for us in Africa.

There is nothing new in South Africa's apartheid ideas, but South Africa is unique in this: the ideas not only survive in our modern age but are stubbornly defended, extended, and bolstered up by legislation at the time when, in the major part of the world, they are now largely historical and are either being shamefacedly hidden behind concealing formulations or are being steadily scrapped. These ideas survive in South Africa because those who sponsor them profit from them. They provide moral whitewash for the conditions which exist in the country: for the fact that the country is ruled exclusively by a white government elected by an exclusively white electorate which is a privileged minority; for the fact that eighty-seven percent of the land and all the best agricultural land within reach of town, market, and railways are reserved for white ownership and occupation, and now through the recent Group Areas legislation nonwhites are losing more land to white greed; for the fact that all skilled and highly paid jobs are for whites only; for the fact that all universities of any academic merit are exclusively preserves of whites; for the fact that the education of every white child costs about £64 per year while that of an African child costs about £9 per year and that of an Indian child or colored child costs about £20 per year; for the fact that white education is universal and compulsory up to the age of sixteen, while education for the nonwhite children is scarce and inadequate; and for the fact that almost one million Africans a year are arrested and jailed or fined for breaches of innumerable pass and permit laws, which do not apply to whites.

I could carry on in this strain and talk on every facet of South African life from the cradle to the grave. But these facts today are becoming known to all the world. A fierce spotlight of world attention has been thrown on them. Try as our government and its apologists will, with honeyed words about "separate development" and eventual "independence" in so-called "Bantu homelands," nothing can conceal the reality of South African conditions. I, as a Christian, have always felt that there is one thing above all about "apartheid" or "separate development" that is unforgivable. It seems utterly indifferent to the suffering of individual persons, who lose their land, their homes, their jobs, in the pursuit of what is surely the most terrible dream in the world. This terrible dream is not held on to by a crackpot group on the fringe of society or by Ku Klux Klansmen, of whom we have a sprinkling. It is the deliberate policy of a government, supported actively by a large part of the white population and tolerated passively by an overwhelming white majority, but now fortunately rejected by an encouraging white minority who have thrown their lot with nonwhites, who are overwhelmingly opposed to so-called separate development. Thus it is that the golden age of Africa's independence is also the dark age of South Africa's decline and retrogression, brought about by men who, when revolutionary changes that entrenched fundamental human rights were taking place in Europe, were closed in on the tip of South Africa—and so missed the wind of progressive change.

In the wake of that decline and retrogression, bitterness between men grows to alarming heights; the economy declines as confidence ebbs away; unemployment rises; government becomes increasingly dictatorial and intolerant of constitutional and legal procedures, increasingly violent and suppressive; there is a constant drive for more policemen, more soldiers, more armaments, banishments without trial, and penal whippings. All the trappings of medieval backwardness and cruelty come to the fore. Education is being reduced to an instrument of subtle indoctrination; slanted and biased reporting in the organs of public information, a creeping censorship, book banning, and blacklisting—all these spread their shadows over the land. This is South Africa today, in the age of Africa's greatness.

But beneath the surface there is a spirit of defiance. The people of South Africa have never been a docile lot, least of all the African people. We have a long tradition of struggle for our national rights, reaching back to the very beginnings of white settlement and conquest 300 years ago. Our history is one of opposition to domination, of protest and refusal to submit to tyranny. Consider some of our great names: the great warrior and nation builder Shaka, who welded tribes together into the Zulu nation from which I spring; Moshoeshoe, the statesman and nation-builder who fathered the Basuto nation and placed Basutoland beyond the reach of the claws of the South African whites; Hintsa of the Xosas, who chose death rather than surrender his territory to white invaders. All these and other royal names, as well as other great chieftains, resisted manfully white intrusion. Consider also the sturdiness of the stock that nurtured the foregoing great names. I refer to our forbears, who, in trekking from the north to the southernmost tip of Africa centuries ago, braved rivers that are perennially swollen; hacked their way through treacherous jungle and forest; survived the plagues of the then untamed lethal diseases of a multifarious nature that abounded in Equatorial Africa; and wrested themselves from the gaping mouths of the beasts of prey. They endured it all. They settled in these parts of Africa to build a future worthwhile for us, their offspring. While the social and political conditions have changed and the problems we face are different, we too, their progeny, find ourselves facing a situation where we have to struggle for our very survival as human beings. Although methods of struggle may differ from time to time, the universal human strivings for liberty remain unchanged. We, in our situation, have chosen the path of non-violence of our own volition. Along this path we have organized many heroic campaigns. All the strength of progressive leadership in South Africa, all my life and strength, have been given to the pursuance of this method, in an attempt to avert disaster in the interests of South Africa, and [we] have bravely paid the penalties for it.

4

Violence and Armed Struggle

20

DAVID RAMOHOASE

The Sharpeville Massacre of March 21, 1960
1996

David Ramohoase, a victim of the shootings at Sharpeville in 1960, testified to the Truth and Reconciliation Commission (TRC) thirty-six years later about his experiences at the PAC-organized protest against the pass laws. A crowd of several thousand had gathered at the Sharpeville police station. Police opened fire, shooting sixty-nine unarmed protesters. Following Sharpeville, the apartheid authorities declared a state of emergency, detained thousands of activists, and banned the PAC and ANC. The ANC gave Sharpeville as the reason for its embarking on an armed struggle. Ramohoase's perspective is personal, that of a nonpoliticized protester who was at the station simply because he did not like the pass system.

COMMISSIONER: Thank you very much. Utata[1] you are also going to tell us about what happened on that fateful day . . . in 1960. Please take your time and tell us your story.

MR DAVID RAMOHOASE: In 1960 we were on our way to work and people stopped us. You know they just stopped us from going to work and we asked them what to do. They said no, we are heading for the police station today. We asked them what are you going to do there, they said

[1]An honorific title for an elderly man.

Testimony of David Ramohoase, Truth and Reconciliation Commission, Sebokeng, August 5, 1996, www.justice.gov.za/trc/hrvtrans/sebokeng/seb902.htm.

no we are going to enquire about our pass. And after a few minutes we decided to go to the police station. I wanted to go and listen to this issue about passes. When we arrived there we spent some few minutes sitting, you know there was a large crowd of people going just up and down. Between one and two o'clock after a long time that we have been there a car drove in, a very small car. It drove into the police station premise but the armoured vehicles, the saracens, had already been there already. Two of them approached from the south, they got into the police station premise and they faced to the west. That is the site where most of the people were gathered. They faced towards the people. Most of the people were just behind the fence. This white car drove in and a man jumped out of the car, a white person, and he had a very short stick in his hand and then he had a band on his head. He had this stick, you know he just dropped his stick and then he said "Shoot." I don't know what happened because it was now chaos. People were lying on the ground. At the time while I was on the ground a person who was shot lying [next] to me said things are bad please lie down, don't try to raise your head otherwise they are going to shoot you. When the ambulances and the police vans arrived we were taken—and I was taken by a municipal van to the Vereeniging Hospital. That is what I witnessed on that 21st day. The day of March. We were treated at the Vereeniging Hospital. I spent three months there and a few days. I can't remember but three months went by. I was shot on the right leg just above the knee. It was broken in two. The bone was just broken and even now if I can show you you will see that I was badly injured. That is the experience that I have been through because I didn't know exactly what was happening. . . .

COMMISSIONER: Were you a member of any political organisation at the time and did you understand what the protest was all about?

MR DAVID RAMOHOASE: I didn't know anything at that stage. I wasn't even belonging to any political organisation. I only heard about the existence but I never had any interest to join any. I was just an ordinary person.

COMMISSIONER: Can you just tell us before the policeman gave the order to shoot how many people do you think had gathered on that day?

MR DAVID RAMOHOASE: It was a large group, 300 to 400 people. I cannot estimate exactly the number but it was a large group. It was a group like the one you see in front of you here. Maybe even more than the group here.

COMMISSIONER: Utata you say that after you fell and somebody said to you keep your head down, you also heard policemen coming around and saying—and finishing some people off. Can you please tell us what you mean by that.

MR DAVID RAMOHOASE: What I saw with my eyes the time I tried to raise my head I was trying to look so that I can find my way out. The person who was lying next to me said please don't raise your head, these people will come and finish us off because they are shooting. As I was lying the police were turning people down and you would see them turning this person down and then you know you would see a person just throwing his hands and then I would be shocked as to what was happening. And they would go to the next but I couldn't see who these police were. They would go to the next one and then they would turn him and you would see this person you know just getting dumped, you know we didn't know actually what were they doing to the people. But according to our minds they were doing something to the people. Every time they go the next person you would see this person throwing his hands. They also came to me, they asked me where have we shot you. And I showed them my knee. I said here and they just passed. He said Africa is no longer a thumb facing upwards [the PAC symbol], it is a thumb facing downwards now. . . .

QUESTION: Utata Ramohoase, I would like you to assist the Commission to get a picture of the mood of the people before the police started shooting. . . .

MR DAVID RAMOHOASE: It was a very sunny day. Many young men were gathering holding their umbrellas in their hands, they were singing Nkosi Sikileli. . . . Now this white man just gave a sign and shots were fired. We were still at the sing.

QUESTION: . . . Did people try to fight back, were they armed, please if you can just give us a clear picture of the people's reaction.

MR DAVID RAMOHOASE: Not even one person was armed. I saw men and women and young men just holding their umbrellas because it was a hot day. Those who might have had guns, maybe they were hidden somewhere but I didn't see anyone carrying any weapon, not even a stick and knobkerrie [a wooden stick with a large knob at the end], not even a knobkerrie. I only saw umbrellas. If one of them had a weapon or you know like a knobkerrie or a spear or a gun I didn't see any. Because I believe that the people wanted to know something about the passes. They were not going there to fight. They were peaceful. They didn't have anything in their hands.

QUESTION: Following that incident I suppose there were burials, funerals and community meetings. Can you assist us as to what went on[?]

Whatever you might have heard of or you might be aware of, people's reaction to what had occurred in the area of Sebokeng.

MR DAVID RAMOHOASE: I think people's emotions were raised high because this incident took many lives and many were injured. Women lost husbands, husbands lost wives and children lost parents. Now the community wasn't supposed to feel happy about this. Even if I wasn't injured I would never feel happy at all about this. It was a very bad thing to happen.

21

NELSON MANDELA

Statement at the Rivonia Trial
1964

In his concluding address at the trial in which he and his nine co-accused were convicted of the attempted armed overthrow of the state and sentenced to life imprisonment, Nelson Mandela spoke of his decision to turn to an armed struggle and of the demands of the ANC. The last paragraph of this famous address became a mantra for Mandela and those who supported him.

I am the First Accused.

I hold a Bachelor's Degree in Arts and practised as an attorney in Johannesburg for a number of years in partnership with Oliver Tambo. I am a convicted prisoner serving five years for leaving the country without a permit and for inciting people to go on strike at the end of May, 1961.

At the outset, I want to say that the suggestion made by the State in its opening that the struggle in South Africa is under the influence of

Nelson R. Mandela, "Statement during the Rivonia Trial," in *From Protest to Challenge: A Documentary History of African Politics in South Africa, 1882–1964*, ed. Thomas Karis and Gwendolyn M. Carter, vol. 3, *Challenge and Violence, 1953–1964*, by Thomas Karis and Gail M. Gerhart (Stanford, Calif.: Hoover Institution, 1977), 771–72, 774–77, 795–96.

foreigners or communists is wholly incorrect. I have done whatever I did, both as an individual and as a leader of my people, because of my experience in South Africa and my own proudly felt African background, and not because of what any outsider might have said.

In my youth in the Transkei I listened to the elders of my tribe telling stories of the old days. Amongst the tales they related to me were those of wars fought by our ancestors in defence of the fatherland. . . . I hoped then that life might offer me the opportunity to serve my people and make my own humble contribution to their freedom struggle. This is what has motivated me in all that I have done in relation to the charges made against me in this case.

Having said this, I must deal immediately and at some length, with the question of violence. Some of the things so far told to the Court are true and some are untrue. I do not, however, deny that I planned sabotage. I did not plan it in a spirit of recklessness, nor because I have any love of violence. I planned it as a result of a calm and sober assessment of the political situation that had arisen after many years of tyranny, exploitation and oppression of my people by the Whites.

I admit immediately that I was one of the persons who helped to form Umkonto We Sizwe [Umkhonto we Sizwe or MK], and that I played a prominent role in its affairs until I was arrested in August, 1962. . . .

In 1960, there was the shooting at Sharpeville, which resulted in the proclamation of a State of Emergency and the declaration of the A.N.C. as an unlawful organization. My colleagues and I, after careful consideration, decided that we would not obey this decree. The African people were not part of the Government and did not make the laws by which they were governed. We believed in the words of the Universal Declaration of Human Rights, that "the will of the people shall be the basis of the authority of the Government," and for us to accept the banning was equivalent to accepting the silencing of the Africans for all time. The A.N.C. refused to dissolve, but instead went underground. We believed it was our duty to preserve this organization which had been built up with almost fifty years of unremitting toil. I have no doubt that no self-respecting White political organization would disband itself if declared illegal by a Government in which it had no say. . . .

In 1960 the Government held a Referendum which led to the establishment of the Republic. Africans, who constituted approximately 70% of the population of South Africa, were not entitled to vote, and were not even consulted about the proposed constitutional change. All of us were apprehensive of our future under the proposed White Republic, and a resolution was taken to hold an All-In African Conference to call for a

National Convention, and to organize mass demonstrations on the eve of the unwanted Republic, if the Government failed to call the Convention. The Conference was attended by Africans of various political persuasions. I was the Secretary of the Conference and undertook to be responsible for organizing the national stay-at-home which was subsequently called to coincide with the declaration of the Republic. As all strikes by Africans are illegal, the person organizing such a strike must avoid arrest. I was chosen to be this person, and consequently I had to leave my home and family and my practice and go into hiding to avoid arrest.

The stay-at-home, in accordance with A.N.C. policy, was to be a peaceful demonstration. Careful instructions were given to organizers and members to avoid any recourse to violence. The Government's answer was to introduce new and harsher laws, to mobilise its armed forces, and to send saracens, armed vehicles and soldiers into the townships in a massive show of force designed to intimidate the people. This was an indication that the Government had decided to rule by force alone, and this decision was a milestone on the road to Umkonto. . . .

What were we, the leaders of our people to do? Were we to give in to the show of force and the implied threat against future action, or were we to fight it, and if so, how? We had no doubt that we had to continue the fight. Anything else would have been abject surrender. Our problem was not whether to fight, but was how to continue the fight. We of the A.N.C. had always stood for a non-racial democracy, and we shrank from any action which might drive the races further apart than they already were. But the hard facts were that fifty years of non-violence had brought the African people nothing but more and more repressive legislation, and fewer and fewer rights. It may not be easy for this Court to understand, but it is a fact that for a long time the people had been talking of violence — of the day when they would fight the White man and win back their country, and we, the leaders of the A.N.C., had nevertheless always prevailed upon them to avoid violence and to pursue peaceful methods. When some of us discussed this in May and June of 1961, it could not be denied that our policy to achieve a non-racial state by non-violence had achieved nothing, and that our followers were beginning to lose confidence in this policy and were developing disturbing ideas of terrorism.

It must not be forgotten that by this time violence had, in fact, become a feature of the South African political scene. There had been violence in 1957 when the women of Zeerust were ordered to carry passes; there was violence in 1958 with the enforcement of cattle culling in Sekhukuniland; there was violence in 1959 when the people of Cato Manor protested against Pass raids; there was violence in 1960 when the Government attempted to impose Bantu Authorities in Pondoland. Thirty-nine Africans died in these disturbances. In 1961 there had been riots in Warmbaths, and all this time the Transkei had been a seething mass of unrest. Each disturbance pointed clearly to the inevitable growth among Africans of the belief that violence was the only way out—it showed that a Government which uses force to maintain its rule teaches the oppressed to use force to oppose it. Already small groups had arisen in the urban areas and were spontaneously making plans for violent forms of political struggle. There now arose a danger that these groups would adopt terrorism against Africans, as well as Whites, if not properly directed. Particularly disturbing was the type of violence engendered in places such as Zeerust, Sekhukhuniland and Pondoland amongst Africans. It was increasingly taking the form, not of struggle against the Government—though this is what prompted it—but of civil strife amongst themselves, conducted in such a way that it could not hope to achieve anything other than a loss of life and bitterness.

At the beginning of June, 1961, after a long and anxious assessment of the South African situation, I, and some colleagues, came to the conclusion that as violence in this country was inevitable, it would be unrealistic and wrong for African leaders to continue preaching peace and non-violence at a time when the Government met our peaceful demands with force. This conclusion was not easily arrived at. It was only when all else had failed, when all channels of peaceful protest had been barred to us, that the decision was made to embark on violent forms of political struggle, and to form Umkonto We Sizwe. We did so not because we desired such a course, but solely because the Government had left us with no other choice. In the Manifesto of Umkonto published on the 16th December, 1961, . . . we said:—

"The time comes in the life of any nation when there remain only two choices—submit or fight. That time has now come to South Africa. We shall not submit and we have no choice but to hit back by all means in our power in defence of our people, our future and our freedom." . . .

Africans want to be paid a living wage. Africans want to perform work which they are capable of doing, and not work which the Government declares them to be capable of. Africans want to be allowed to live where they obtain work, and not be endorsed out of an area because they were not born there. Africans want to be allowed to own land in places where they work, and not to be obliged to live in rented houses which they can never call their own. Africans want to be part of the general population, and not confined to living in their own ghettos. African men want to have their wives and children live with them where they work, and not be forced into an unnatural existence in men's hostels. African women want to be with their men folk and not be left permanently widowed in the reserves. Africans want to be allowed out after 11 o'clock at night and not to be confined to their rooms like little children. Africans want to be allowed to travel in their own country and to seek work where they want to and not where the Labour Bureau tells them to. Africans want a just share in the whole of South Africa; they want security and a stake in society.

Above all, we want equal political rights, because without them our disabilities will be permanent. I know this sounds revolutionary to the Whites in this country, because the majority of voters will be Africans. This makes the White man fear democracy. But this fear cannot be allowed to stand in the way of the only solution which will guarantee racial harmony and freedom for all. It is not true that the enfranchisement of all will result in racial domination. Political division, based on colour, is entirely artificial and, when it disappears, so will the domination of one colour group by another. The A.N.C. has spent half a century fighting against racialism. When it triumphs it will not change that policy.

This then is what the A.N.C. is fighting. Their struggle is a truly national one. It is a struggle of the African people, inspired by their own suffering and their own experience. It is a struggle for the right to live.

During my lifetime I have dedicated myself to this struggle of the African people. I have fought against White domination, and I have fought against Black domination. I have cherished the ideal of a democratic and free society in which all persons live together in harmony and with equal opportunities. It is an ideal which I hope to live for and to achieve. But if needs be, it is an ideal for which I am prepared to die.

22

ANC RADIO FREEDOM

You Will Learn How to Use a Gun
1969?

Radio Freedom was the ANC's shortwave radio station that broadcast to South Africa from Lusaka, Zambia. This is one of the early broadcasts from exile, which reflects the ANC's revolutionary rhetoric, even as the organization collapsed in South Africa. Calls for violent insurrection inside the country, different from the program of sabotage advocated by Nelson Mandela, were hardly realistic given the extent of the apartheid repression and the weakness of the ANC within the country.

VOICE: This is the African National Congress. This is the African National Congress. This is the Voice of Freedom. The ANC speaks to you! Afrika! Mayibuye!

SINGING OF THE NATIONAL ANTHEM (NKOSI SIKELELE AFRIKA AND MORENA BOLOKA)

VOICE: The time has come. This Government of slavery, this Government of oppression, this Apartheid monster must be removed from power and crushed by the People! It must be removed by force! They will never stop the pass raids, the arrests, the beatings, the killings—they will continue to drive us out of our homes like dogs and send us to rot in the so-called Bantu homelands, they will continue to pay us miserable wages, and treat us as their beasts of burden until the day we beat them up and crush white rule! This land of ours was taken away by bloodshed, we will regain it by bloodshed. Sons and daughters of Afrika, you in your millions who have toiled to make this country rich,

"Transcription of ANC Radio Freedom Broadcast, 1969?," in Thomas G. Karis and Gail M. Gerhart, *From Protest to Challenge: A Documentary History of African Politics in South Africa, 1882–1990,* vol. 5, *Nadir and Resurgence, 1964–1979* (Bloomington: Indiana University Press, 1997), 377–80.

the ANC calls upon you: Never submit to white oppression; never give up the Freedom struggle; find ways of organising those around you—the African National Congress calls you to be ready—to be ready for war! You will soon learn how to make a petrol bomb. You will also learn how to shoot a gun. You must learn how to outwit the enemy, his spies and informers, and organise those around you. We are many, they are few. Our Coloured and Indian brothers must do the same. You must organise your people to fight the ghettoes and all the racial laws and in support of the armed struggle. We say to the enemy that we will not be bluffed by your toy parliaments like Matanzima's [Chief Mantanzima was head of the Transkei Bantustan], like the Coloured Council and like the Indian Council. We want Freedom now! REAL FREEDOM! But the whites will not give it to us. We have to take it. We have to take it by violence. . . . We must resist the Matanzima stooges, we must resist the Bantu Authorities Act in the countryside. We want our land back. Our young men with guns will fight for it in the countryside. They will deal with the stooges and informers, the police and the white soldiers. Our people in the countryside must be told of their coming. They must hide and feed our freedom fighters, they must make their path easy and the enemy's path hard. The African National Congress calls upon our people to prepare for guerrilla warfare, the People's War of Liberation, NOW! Guerrilla war has brought victory to the people of Algeria, to the people of Cuba, to the people of Vietnam. Those people did not have big armies. They were like us. Guerrilla fighters organise themselves in small groups. Suddenly when the enemy is not expecting them, they attack. They kill and grab the guns and disappear. You sons and daughters of the soil, you must consider yourselves as soldiers in the guerrilla war. There are many ways to be a freedom fighter. . . . The African National Congress calls on all the oppressed people to organise and struggle and prepare to fight in the towns and countryside. Our brave men of Umkonto we Sizwe have shown the way. They fought heroically in Zimbabwe. They will fight in South Africa. You must start to find places where you can hide the weapons you might come across. You must have secret addresses of your reliable friends who will agree to hide you or your weapons or other freedom fighters. You must be ready to sacrifice. You must start now to find hiding places. The countryside, the bush, the forest, the mountain—these will also become your secret addresses. The time has come. The African National Congress calls upon you to organise and to prepare. Death to racialism! Mayibuy' Afrika! Amandla! Ke Nako Zemk' inkomo magwala ndini!

AyiHlome!
[Now is the time. The cattle are being stolen, you cowards! Be armed!]

SINGING OF FREEDOM SONGS.

23

DENNIS BRUTUS

On the Island

1973

*Coloured, Indian, and African political prisoners were incarcerated with
Nelson Mandela and those convicted in the Rivonia Trial on Robben
Island, off the coast of Cape Town. Robben Island became a symbol of
apartheid. In this selection, Dennis Brutus, of mixed race and classified
by apartheid authorities as coloured, describes the island in the 1960s
and 1970s, when prisoners were isolated and subjected to forced labor in the
lime quarry. In later years, as the number of political prisoners increased,
Robben Island spawned solidarity within the liberation movement.*

1

Cement-grey floors and walls
cement-grey days
cement-grey time
and a grey susurration
as of seas breaking
winds blowing
and rains drizzling

A barred existence
so that one did not need to look
at doors or windows

Dennis Brutus, "On the Island," in *A Simple Lust* (London: Heinemann, 1973), 71.

to know that they were sundered by bars
and one locked in a grey gelid stream
of unmoving time.

2

When the rain came
it came in a quick moving squall
moving across the island
murmuring from afar
then drumming on the roof
then marching fading away.

And sometimes one mistook
the weary tramp of feet
as the men came shuffling from the quarry
white-dust-filmed and shambling
for the rain
that came and drummed and marched away.

24

OLIVER TAMBO

A Future Free of Exploitation
1977

Oliver Tambo, a collaborator of Nelson Mandela's, escaped South Africa to head the ANC in exile from 1967 to 1990. Under his leadership, the armed wing grew, as did relations with Eastern bloc countries (although Tambo was not a communist). ANC and South African Communist Party (SACP) leaders allied South Africa's struggle with anticolonial struggles across southern Africa. At the first congress of the Movimento

Oliver R. Tambo, "A Future Free of Exploitation," in *Mandela, Tambo, and the African National Congress: The Struggle against Apartheid; A Documentary History, 1948–1990*, ed. Sheridan Johns and R. Hunt Davis Jr. (New York: Oxford University Press, 1991), 235–36.

Popular de Libertação de Angola (Popular Movement for the Liberation of Angola, or MPLA), which led Angola after it declared its independence from Portugal, Tambo linked the end of apartheid to international socialist revolution. The ANC would join in the Angolan civil war and establish bases in Angola, but in the 1970s it was cut off from struggles within South Africa.

This first Congress of MPLA is a victory of the Angolan people. It is also a victory of all the peoples, including the peoples of South Africa, who are pledged to fight for the creation of new socioeconomic systems which will be characterized by the abolition of exploitation of man by man through ownership of productive wealth by the people themselves; characterized as well by the self-government of the ordinary working people through the institution of popular power and characterized also by a commitment to strive for a world that has been rid of the parasites that have imposed on all of us; fascism, racism, and apartheid, deprivation and backwardness, ignorance, superstition, and destructive wars.

Angola's orientation towards the social emancipation of her people has therefore, like Mozambique, brought to the fore, in our region, the confrontation between the liberating theory and practice of socialism and the oppressive, exploitative, and antihuman system of capitalism. This latter social system is of course represented, par excellence, by racist South Africa itself. Hence today the open and sharp confrontations between People's Angola and Mozambique on the one side and fascist South Africa and colonial Rhodesia on the other. . . .

These victories have helped to deepen the general crisis of the apartheid colonial system: They have in the actuality of South African politics helped to strengthen the forces of progress and severely weaken the forces of reaction. In that fact lies the fundamental reason for the desperate determination of the Vorster regime to destroy these two people's republics. In that also lies essentially the reason why we of the African National Congress join voices with Comrade President Neto [of Angola] in saying the victory of the Angolan people is indeed truly our own as well.

In the very first hours of its existence, people's Angola had to defend itself against the massive military onslaught of a mature but decaying imperialist system. . . .

The results of that contest have now become a matter of proud historical record. Progress triumphed over reaction, thanks to the heroic sacrifices of the people of Angola, supported by their progressive African allies, by Cuba, the Soviet Union and other socialist countries, and by all peoples advancing towards progress.

What started as a triumphant march by the forces of reaction into the heart of Angola ended up with a deeper crisis for the Vorster regime inside South Africa itself: the humiliating defeat of Vorster's social system for which that army had been created, trained, and armed to defend. The myth of the invincibility of the racist army was destroyed forever. For the fascist regime of John Vorster, whose ultimate and principal means of survival is naked brute force, this was a stunning blow. It proved to our own people, as well as to the more far-seeing sections of the oppressor population, including especially the youth, that in the confrontation with the forces of progress, the fascist state is destined inevitably to lose, wherever that confrontation takes place, but above all, and especially, within South Africa itself.

5

Resistance and Repression: Students, Workers, Women, Clergy, and Conscripts

25

STEPHEN BANTU BIKO

The Definition of Black Consciousness
1971?

A renowned student leader who brought Black Consciousness ideas to the forefront of South African resistance politics during the 1970s, Stephen Bantu (Steve) Biko was killed while detained by the police in 1977. He established Black Consciousness as the leading student ideology of the decade. This paper was produced for a black student leadership conference, probably in December 1971.

We have in our policy manifesto defined blacks as those who are by law or tradition politically, economically and socially discriminated against as a group in the South African society and identifying themselves as a unit in the struggle towards the realisation of their aspirations.

This definition illustrates to us a number of things:

1. Being black is not a matter of pigmentation—being black is a reflection of a mental attitude.

2. Merely by describing yourself as black you have started on a road towards emancipation, you have committed yourself to

Steve Biko, "The Definition of Black Consciousness," in *I Write What I Like* (London: Bowerdean, 1978), 48–51.

fight against all forces that seek to use your blackness as a stamp that marks you out as a subservient being.

From the above observations therefore, we can see that the term black is not necessarily all-inclusive; i.e. the fact we are all *not white* does not necessarily mean that we are all *black*. Non-whites do exist and will continue to exist and will continue to exist for quite a long time. If one's aspiration is whiteness but his pigmentation makes attainment of this impossible, then that person is a non-white. Any man who calls a white man "Baas," any man who serves in the police force or Security Branch is *ipso facto* a non-white. Black people—real black people—are those who can manage to hold their heads high in defiance rather than willingly surrender their souls to the white man.

Briefly defined therefore, Black Consciousness is in essence the realisation by the black man of the need to rally together with his brothers around the cause of their operation—the blackness of their skin—and to operate as a group in order to rid themselves of the shackles that bind them to perpetual servitude. It seeks to demonstrate the lie that black is an aberration from the "normal" which is white. It is a manifestation of a new realisation that by seeking to run away from themselves and to emulate the white man, blacks are insulting the intelligence of whoever created them black. Black Consciousness therefore, takes cognizance of the deliberateness of God's plan in creating black people black. It seeks to infuse the black community with a new-found pride in themselves, their efforts, their value systems, their culture, their religion and their outlook to life.

The interrelationship between the consciousness of the self and the emancipatory programme is of paramount importance. Blacks no longer seek to reform the system because so doing implies acceptance of the major points around which the system revolves. Blacks are out to completely transform the system and to make of it what they wish. Such a major undertaking can only be realised in an atmosphere where people are convinced of the truth inherent in their stand. Liberation therefore, is of paramount importance in the concept of Black Consciousness, for we cannot be conscious of ourselves and yet remain in bondage. We want to attain the envisioned self which is a free self.

The surge towards Black Consciousness is a phenomenon that has manifested itself throughout the so-called Third World. There is no doubt that discrimination against the black man the world over fetches its origin from the exploitative attitude of the white man. Colonisation of white countries by whites has throughout history resulted in nothing more sinister than mere cultural or geographical fusion at worst, or language bastardisation at best. It is true that the history of weaker nations is shaped by bigger nations, but nowhere in the world today do we see whites exploiting whites on a scale even remotely similar to what is happening in South Africa. Hence, one is forced to conclude that it is not coincidence that black people are exploited. It was a deliberate plan which has culminated in even so-called black independent countries not attaining any real independence.

With this background in mind we are forced, therefore, to believe that it is a case of *haves* against *have-nots* where whites have been deliberately made *haves* and blacks *have-nots*. There is for instance no worker in the classical sense among whites in South Africa, for even the most downtrodden white worker still has a lot to lose if the system is changed. He is protected by several laws against competition at work from the majority. He has a vote and he uses it to return the Nationalist Government to power because he sees them as the only people who, through job reservation laws, are bent on looking after his interests against competition with the "Natives."

It should therefore be accepted that an analysis of our situation in terms of one's colour at once takes care of the greatest single determinant for political action—i.e. colour—while also validly describing the blacks as the only real workers in South Africa. It immediately kills all suggestions that there could ever be effective rapport between the real workers, i.e. blacks, and the privileged white workers since we have shown that the latter are the greatest supporters of the system. True enough, the system has allowed so dangerous an anti-black attitude to build up amongst whites that it is taken as almost sin to be black and hence the poor whites, who are economically nearest to the blacks, demonstrate the distance between themselves and the blacks by an exaggerated reactionary attitude towards blacks. Hence the greatest anti-black feeling is to be found amongst the very poor whites whom the Class Theory calls upon to be with black workers in the struggle for emancipation. This is the kind of twisted logic that the Black Consciousness approach seeks to eradicate.

In terms of the Black Consciousness approach we recognise the existence of one major force in South Africa. This is White Racism. It is the one force against which all of us are pitted. It works with unnerving totality, featuring both on the offensive and in our defence. Its greatest ally to date has been the refusal by us to club together as blacks because we are told to do so would be racialist. So, while we progressively lose ourselves in a world of colourlessness and amorphous common humanity, whites are deriving pleasure and security in entrenching white racism and further exploiting the minds and bodies of the unsuspecting black masses. Their agents are ever present amongst us, telling us that it is immoral to withdraw into a cocoon, that dialogue is the answer to our problem and that it is unfortunate that there is white racism in some quarters but you must understand that things are changing. These in fact are the greatest racists for they refuse to credit us with any intelligence to know what we want. Their intentions are obvious; they want to be barometers by which the rest of the white society can measure feelings in the black world. This then is what makes us believe that white power presents itself as a totality not only provoking us but also controlling our response to the provocation. This is an important point to note because it is often missed by those who believe that there are a few good whites. Sure there are a few good whites just as much as there are a few bad blacks.

However what we are concerned here with is group attitudes and group politics. The exception does not make a lie of the rule—it merely substantiates it.

26

Sam Nzima with His Photo of Hector Pieterson
June 16, 1976

In 1976 students protested against Bantu education, and in particular against the introduction of Afrikaans as a language medium of instruction alongside English. The uprising in Soweto, the largest township outside Johannesburg, was the most bitterly fought. A photograph of one of the first killed, Hector Pieterson—carried by an eighteen-year-old schoolboy and accompanied by his sister—became an iconic image of the uprising and of the brutality of apartheid in general. At the time, the photographer, Sam Nzima, worked at The World *newspaper. After taking the photograph, he fled to a rural area and was hounded for years by the apartheid security police.*

Denis Farrell / AP Images.

27

KHOTSO SEATLHOLO

Soweto Students' Representative Council Press Release

October 29, 1976

In this press release, one of the student leaders of the Soweto uprising explains its causes. The influence of Black Consciousness and rebellion against the older generation, including their parents and the previous leaders of the liberation movement, is apparent.

"Press Release by Khotso Seatlholo, Chairman of the Soweto Students' Representative Council, October 29, 1976," in Thomas G. Karis and Gail M. Gerhart, *From Protest to Challenge: A Documentary History of African Politics in South Africa, 1882–1990*, vol. 5, *Nadir and Resurgence, 1964–1979* (Bloomington: Indiana University Press, 1997), 587–88.

Many people, including the Vorster Government, [Minister of Justice] Jimmy Kruger's police and some fascist Government's secret agents, have attributed the present unrests in Soweto and all over the country, to the ANC, PAC or some subversive Communist organisations. Some Government officials have even had the guts to point a finger at the Black Consciousness movements who have to date operated overboard in broad daylight. If this be true that the above organisations are the cause of upheavals, then we take off our hats for the South African Security force. They seem to be efficiently inefficient in their detective work. They deserve a Noble Price [*sic*] for being too fast to accuse, and faster to find a scapegoat.

We tried to locate symptoms of the above revolutionary organisations, we failed. We worked hard to unearth the communist agitators who caused so much loss of life and bloodshed in our peaceful Black community, we found none. Then our main task was to find the real cause of the unrest and riots all over the country. We found it. It was glaring right into our face—it was the *WHITE FASCIST MINORITY GOVERNMENT OF JOHN VORSTER* and his gang of pro-nazi Ministers.

It is a pity that Mr Kruger and his security police could not see this monstrous beam in his regime's eye and racial policies. When we were born, we found our fathers struggling under the yoke of oppression. We found ourselves ushered into a socio-economic and political situation which was neither of our father's [*sic*] nor of our making. Black people have never been consulted in the making of laws that are today oppressing us; and have made South Africa the stink-cat (meerkat) of the world. We cannot afford to be ostracised from the world community because of no fault of our own. We strongly reject the subservient heritage that our fathers have handed down to us. Our fathers stood up to speak and fight for their rights, they were given Robben Island as eternal place of residence. Their peaceful pleas were answered with ruthless violent acts of suppression, and they lived on as a politically crippled nation.

We came. We saw. We judged and ACTED or REACTED to the whole system of oppression discriminatory racist laws. We refuse to bend down that the White man can ride on our back. We have the full right to stand up erect and reject the whole system of apartheid. We cannot accept it, as our fathers did. We are neither carbon nor duplicate copies of our fathers. Where they failed we shall succeed. The mistakes they made shall never be repeated. They carried the struggle up to where they could. We are very grateful to them. But now, the struggle is ours. The ball of liberation is in our hands. The Black student shall, fearlessly, stand up and take arms against a political system which is stinking with immoral policies that we have found distasteful and unacceptable to us. We shall rise up and destroy a political ideology that is designed to keep us in a perpetual state of oppression and subserviency. We shall oppose the economic system that is keeping us in non-ending state of poverty. We shall not stand a social system of discrimination that has become an insult to our human dignity. We shall reject the whole system of Bantu Education whose aim is to reduce us, mentally and physically, into "hewers of wood and drawers of water" for the White racist monsters. Our whole "being" rebels against the whole South African system of existence, the system of apartheid that is killing us psychologically and physically. The type of education we receive is like poison that is destroying our minds.

It is reducing us into intellectual cripples that cannot take seat within the World community of academics. It is killing inherent sense of creation in us and thus, it is frustrating us.

Twenty years ago, when Bantu Education was introduced, our fathers said: "half a loaf is better than no loaf." But we say: "half a Gram of poison is just as killing as the whole gram." Thus we strongly refuse to swallow this type of Education that is designed to make us slaves in the country of our birth.

The Afrikaans question that made us to stand together, as students, in one Solidarity to voice our grievances, was just but [the] "Achilles heel" in the whole system of Bantu Education. The enforcement of Afrikaans as a medium of instruction was the last straw on the camel's back. We wish to remind the government that it was the extra charge of a tickey (3d) that broke the British Empire (Boston Tea Party). In the same manner, through the rejection of Afrikaans we are prepared to break the spine of the whole immoral White Apartheid Empire. Morality and the World is on our side. Black Students are determined to die for the Fatherland, the land of AZANIA.[1] The White fascist regime shall be blamed for all the blood shed and misery that shall take place in this country.

[1]Name for South Africa popular in the Black Consciousness movement.

28

FRENE GINWALA

National Liberation and Women's Liberation
1986

Part of the generation of South Africans of Indian descent who became influential members of the ANC, Frene Ginwala fled South Africa following the arrests of the ANC leadership. A leading intellectual and an advocate for women's liberation, she also helped build the ANC in exile. After apartheid, she was a member of parliament and Speaker of the National Assembly. In this interview, Ginwala addresses the relationship of women's liberation to national liberation.

In an official ANC publication it was stated that: "We must start now (if we have not started) to free ourselves from 'male chauvinism' and its counterpart 'feminism.'" Can you explain what this means?

... Unlike some Western interpretations of feminism, the ANC does not see women's liberation in isolation from other forms of oppression in society. If an entire society is oppressed, then to talk of women's liberation in isolation is negative. In South Africa the prime issue is apartheid and national liberation. So to argue that African women should concentrate on and form an isolated feminist movement, focusing on issues of women in their narrowest sense, implies African women must fight so that they can be equally oppressed with African men.

National liberation addresses many issues. What guarantees are there that the liberation of women, the question of male chauvinism as you put it, does not get lost or postponed in the struggle for national liberation?

There is no guarantee in the national liberation struggle. The only guarantee is for women to be involved and make sure their demands are forcefully raised and dealt with. There will never be guarantees, even if clauses are written into constitutions. The danger exists that the issues will not be taken up. . . . I believe that liberation can only be achieved by women themselves, by getting involved. . . . The strength of women's

"ANC Women: Their Strength in the Struggle," *WIP*, November 1986, 10–11, 14.

organisation will determine how and when women's emancipation takes place. . . .

What do you think is specific to women in South African society?
People often ask why pick on South Africa when there are many other oppressive systems? But apartheid is unique in its oppression of women. It is one of the most institutionally organised systems of oppression which has horrific consequences in terms of women's rights, health and social conditions. . . .

But women are also oppressed by their own men, not just apartheid.
Yes, it is not only apartheid, but questions usually focus on the oppression of women in black society. One must also ask how liberated white South African women are within their own social and cultural environment? . . . White women should realize their liberation lies in the national liberation movement. For it is the only organisation in South Africa, black or white, which deals with the issue of women's liberation in its proper context.

29

NATIONAL UNION OF METALWORKERS OF SOUTH AFRICA

Trade Unions and Political Direction

December 1987

In this paper on the political involvement of trade unions, the National Union of Metalworkers of South Africa (NUMSA) discusses Congress of South African Trade Unions (COSATU) support for the national liberation struggle in relation to the campaigns for the working class and to build socialism. COSATU, together with the ANC and SACP, had become

"'Trade Unions and Political Direction,' National Union of Metalworkers (NUMSA) Discussion Paper, December 1987 (abridged)," in Gail M. Gerhart and Clive L. Glaser, *From Protest to Challenge: A Documentary History of African Politics in South Africa, 1882–1990*, vol. 6, *Challenge and Victory, 1980–1990* (Bloomington: Indiana University Press, 2010), 485–87.

part of the Tripartite Alliance against apartheid. This alliance made it unclear as to whether COSATU would give priority to workers' rights and wages in relation to national liberation.

The aim of this paper is to address the question: "WHAT SHOULD BE THE POLITICAL DIRECTION OF OUR UNION IN THE CURRENT SOUTH AFRICAN SITUATION?"

The full answer to this question however will have to come through discussion and debate at all levels of our organisation. This paper only aims to begin that debate. . . .

COSATU Direction

When COSATU was formed at the end of 1985 the office bearers felt that it was important for COSATU to be very much involved in the political struggle in our country. They argued that the members of COSATU themselves were pushing the political struggle and strongly supported political organisations especially the UDF and ANC. They said that if COSATU was not respected politically by all groups then it would be ignored and members would lose faith in the organisation. We believe these beliefs of the COSATU leadership were largely correct.

The COSATU leadership therefore decided to make a lot of public political statements in the newspapers, at meeting[s], at funerals etc. Soon afterwards they went to meet the ANC and issued a communique saying that COSATU was committed to struggling for a non-racial South Africa under the leadership of the ANC. Here we believe that the COSATU leadership made some mistakes because:

i) they did not get mandates from the unions and their members to say many of the things in the newspapers and at meetings and at funerals.

ii) they should have got a very clear mandate to meet the ANC and should not have issued a statement until they had fully discussed their meeting inside COSATU first.

iii) they should not have agreed to COSATU struggling under the leadership of the ANC. They should have made it clear that COSATU, in terms of its own policies, would struggle together with other progressive organisations but independently under its own leadership.

By themselves these mistakes may not appear to be very great but they have certainly created other problems for the Federation. For example:

i) those within the Federation who supported the ANC believed that since COSATU was now operating under the leadership of the ANC there was no room for the other workers who did not fully support the ANC. Workers who expressed different views were threatened and invitations to meet other political organisations were refused.

ii) some unions expected that it was not necessary to get full and proper mandates on all issues from workers and COSATU made some bad errors like the July 14th Stay-Away.

iii) many strong personal attacks were made against people like [Chief M. G.] Buthelezi, which created many problems for unionists and members in Natal when there were in fact better ways to fight Inkatha and UWUSA [United Workers' Union of SA].

As a result of these problems (and other problems as well) COSATU was not able to consolidate itself as an organisation. Most regions are not operating properly. Also COSATU has not learnt to campaign effectively and operate independently and to analyse its mistakes openly and constructively. The question may be raised as to why the COSATU leadership made these mistakes. This paper will not try and answer that question but it is clearly something for members to discuss if they wish.

What we believe is important is for us to learn from those mistakes and to push COSATU also to learn from their mistakes because we are a part of the Federation and we are certainly committed to seeing it survive and grow to be [the] most effective Federation this country has ever seen.

The Road Forward

There can surely be no question of the fact that workers in the trade unions (the organised working class) must be part of the national liberation. If we were not actively part of this struggle then we would not be properly representing the aspirations of our members who want an end to apartheid, who want the right to vote, who want the equal rights etc. But we should ask two further questions:—

i) do our members want more than just an end to apartheid—are they in fact calling for socialism?

ii) do our members want their trade unions to be put under the control of any political party?

If our members are calling for socialism and if they wish their trade unions to maintain their independence (which we believe is the case) then we have a duty to follow those instructions. This means firstly that we must start building for socialism and secondly that we must establish the independence of COSATU within the national liberation struggle. . . . We should be free to choose which groups we wish to unite with and which we wish to reject. No other organisation should be allowed to dictate to us whom our allies should be. If we adopt this *programme of action* which involves building democratic mass based trade unions and community organisations and participating in the national liberation struggle with other organisations on the basis of UNITY IN ACTION, INDEPENDENCE OF ORGANISATIONS AND A COMMITMENT TO SOCIALISM then it is clear that our members must begin to define what they mean by socialism.

This is the responsibility of the working class. A document drawn up by workers spelling out what socialism is would not have to replace other charters like the Freedom Charter. It would simply express what the working class [is] aiming to achieve under socialism.

30

KAIROS: *The Moment of Truth*

1985

Prior to the 1980s, the position of Christian churches in relation to apartheid was ambiguous. Although Catholics and most mainstream Protestants opposed apartheid, they had yet to adopt a united position. Moreover, the Dutch Reformed Church supported apartheid, and many evangelical churches argued that religion should not be mixed with politics. In 1985, 156 clergy from twenty South African Christian denominations committed churches to actively fight apartheid and align themselves with the national liberation movement.

"Challenge to the Church: A Theological Comment on the Political Crisis in South Africa: The Kairos Document, 1985" (Braamfontein: Skotaville Publishers, 1985). Abridged. South African History Online, www.sahistory.org.za/archive/challenge-church-theological -comment-political-crisis-south-africa-kairos-document-1985.

The Moment of Truth

The time has come. The moment of truth has arrived. South Africa has been plunged into a crisis that is shaking the foundations and there is every indication that the crisis has only just begun and that it will deepen and become even more threatening in the months to come. It is the KAIROS or moment of truth not only for apartheid but also for the Church.

We as a group of theologians have been trying to understand the theological significance of this moment in our history. It is serious, very serious. For very many Christians in South Africa this is the KAIROS, the moment of grace and opportunity, the favorable time in which God issues a challenge to decisive action. It is a dangerous time because, if this opportunity is missed, and allowed to pass by, the loss for the Church, for the Gospel and for all the people of South Africa will be immeasurable. Jesus wept over Jerusalem. He wept over the tragedy of the destruction of the city and the massacre of the people that was imminent, "and all because you did not recognize your opportunity (KAIROS) when God offered it" (Lk 19:44).

A crisis is a judgment that brings out the best in some people and the worst in others. A crisis is a moment of truth that shows us up for what we really are. There will be no place to hide and no way of pretending to be what we are not in fact. At this moment in South Africa the Church is about to be shown up for what it really is and no cover-up will be possible.

What the present crisis shows up, although many of us have known it all along, is that the Church is divided. More and more people are now saying that there are in fact two Churches in South Africa—a White Church and a Black Church. Even within the same denomination there are in fact two Churches. In the life and death conflict between different social forces that has come to a head in South Africa today, there are Christians (or at least people who profess to be Christians) on both sides of the conflict—and some who are trying to sit on the fence!

Does this prove that Christian faith has no real meaning or relevance for our times? Does it show that the Bible can be used for any purpose at all? Such problems would be critical enough for the Church in any circumstances but when we also come to see that the conflict in South Africa is between the oppressor and the oppressed, the crisis for the Church as an institution becomes much more acute. Both oppressor and oppressed claim loyalty to the same Church. They are both baptized in the same baptism and participate together in the breaking of the same bread, the same body and blood of Christ. There we sit in the same Church while outside Christian policemen and soldiers are beating up and killing Christian children or torturing Christian prisoners to death while yet other Christians stand by and weakly plead for peace. . . .

Challenge to Action

. . . We are a divided Church precisely because not all the members of our Churches have taken sides against oppression. In other words not all Christians have united themselves with God "who is always on the side of the oppressed" (Ps 103:6). As far as the present crisis is concerned, there is only one way forward to Church unity and that is for those Christians who find themselves on the side of the oppressor or sitting on the fence, to cross over to the other side to be united in faith and action with those who are oppressed. Unity and reconciliation within the Church itself is only possible around God and Jesus Christ who are to be found on the side of the poor and the oppressed. . . .

Christians, if they are not doing so already, must quite simply participate in the struggle for liberation and for a just society. The campaigns of the people, from consumer boycotts to stayaways, need to be supported and encouraged by the Church. Criticism will sometimes be necessary but encouragement and support will also be necessary. In other words the present crisis challenges the whole Church to move beyond a mere "ambulance ministry" to a ministry of involvement and participation. . . .

. . . The evil forces we speak of in baptism must be named. We know what these evil forces are in South Africa today. The unity and sharing we profess in our communion services or Masses must be named. It is the solidarity of the people inviting all to join in the struggle for God's peace in South Africa. The repentance we preach must be named. It is repentance for our share of the guilt for the suffering and oppression in our country. . . .

Once it is established that the present regime has no moral legitimacy and is in fact a tyrannical regime certain things follow for the Church and its activities. In the first place the Church cannot collaborate with tyranny. It cannot or should not do any thing that appears to give legitimacy to a morally illegitimate regime. Secondly, that Church should not only pray for a change of government, it should also mobilize it[s] members in every parish to begin to think and work and plan for a change of government in South Africa. We must begin to look ahead and begin working now with firm hope and faith for a better future. And finally the moral illegitimacy of the apartheid regime means that the Church will have to be involved at times in civil disobedience. A Church that takes its responsibilities seriously in these circumstances will sometimes have to confront and to disobey the State in order to obey God.

DEREK BAUER

P. W. Botha

1987

The visceral images of Derek Bauer depict the political violence of South Africa during the 1980s. In this caricature of Prime Minister P. W. Botha, Bauer conveys the refusal of Botha — and whites in general — to admit to the terror perpetrated by the apartheid regime, in particular that resulting from the extrajudicial powers given to the police after Botha declared a state of emergency in 1985.

Derek Bauer.

DIRK COETZEE

The Murder of Griffiths Mxenge
on 19 November 1981

1996

The state engaged in a violent counterinsurgency initiative throughout the 1980s. One of the most notorious police units, based at Vlakplaas, a farm outside Pretoria, assassinated anti-apartheid activists, undermined the liberation movement through so-called dirty tricks, and turned activists to work as agents for the police. In this transcription of an amnesty hearing before the Truth and Reconciliation Commission (TRC), the first commander of Vlakplaas, Dirk Coetzee, outlines these activities, in particular the murder of anti-apartheid activist and lawyer Griffiths Mxenge. In 1989 Coetzee became a whistle-blower. He was replaced at Vlakplaas by Eugene "Prime Evil" de Kock, who attempted to assassinate him. Although the commanders were white, black policemen or ANC operatives who turned into counterespionage agents (termed Askaris) conducted many of the operations, such as the murder of Griffiths Mxenge.

[Mr Jansen:] Now, what according to you ... did Vlakplaas in fact do ...?

Well, I was only executing orders as far as dirty tricks were concerned, which involved stealing cars, murdering people, harassing people, anything but legal police work or as indicated in the directive....

[Mr Jansen:] What did these dirty tricks entail?

Well, on illegal cross-border raids into neighbouring countries, breaking into the United Nation[s] High Commission office for refugees, for instance as well, and stealing cars, blowing up houses, killing people, blowing up railways lines. Locally in the country abducting so-called activists during the time, getting rid of them....

Testimony of Dirk Coetzee, Truth and Reconciliation Commission, Amnesty Hearing, Durban, November 5, 1996, www.justice.gov.za/trc/amntrans/durban/coetzee1.htm.

[Mr Jansen:] Now, why did you regard such serious transgressions of the ordinary laws of the country as being justified?

Mr Chairman, because the normal, common law of the country, according to our Security Police, was not sufficient to deal effectively with the revolutionary total onslaught, and in a quote—I don't think I can put it better than a quote from Mr Williamson, who was seen as our expert on terrorist matters, when he said . . . ,

"Law enforcement officers, such as members of the SAP [South African Police] and other organs of the Security Forces understand that the RSA [Republic of South Africa] is faced with a revolutionary onslaught which, if it is ever allowed to succeed, will plunge the southern tip of Africa into chaos."

A quote from Captain Williamson in the October 1981 issue of the police magazine, SAPAMAS, in an article with the title, "Why Spy?" If you would allow me to [I] would just like to mention another quote from this article where he says, in the second—next paragraph,

"Therefore the only real answer is secret operations against the enemy using many of the secret operational methods devised by the communist revolutionaries themselves." . . .

[Mr Jansen:] If we can turn to the Mxenge matter. I think it's a matter of public knowledge that Mr Griffiths Mxenge was killed on the 19th of November 1981. . . . Now, were you involved in his murder? . . . Can you relate to the Committee your involvement in this Mxenge matter? I think if you'd start with your presence in Durban at the time.

Mr Chairman, during November, early November—from early November onwards we were operating as a whole Vlakplaas team. All four teams were operating in the Durban area on instructions, and as usual I reported to Brigadier van Hoven's office as officer commanding every morning at half past seven, and every afternoon at 4 o'clock for debriefing and briefing. A few days before the 19th of November, on a morning briefing, he asked me to make a plan with Mr Mxenge. He then in very short terms briefed me that he was an ex Robben Island convict, that he was an attorney, that they were trying to build up a case against him, because he was an acting instructing attorney in all ANC cadres cases who were caught in the country, and that an amount something [like] R200 000,00 [200,000 rand] went through his bank account. He then took me over to the office of then Captain Andy Taylor.

Mr De Jager: Did he add—sorry to interrupt. Did he add anything to the words, "You must make a plan with Mr Mxenge"?

He did, Mr Chairman, in the sense that he said we must not use guns or make him disappear, we must make it look like a robbery.

[Mr Jansen:] Can you continue. What happened thereafter?

He then took me across the passage to Captain Andy Taylor's office, the officer who handled the Mxenge case, who was on his specific case dealing with his surveillance, his phone tapping, et cetera, who then gave me a short description of his office and his house, of how many dogs he had on the premises. If I recall correctly he said it was four.

. . . Captain Andy Taylor also supplied a photograph of Mr Mxenge, which was, I would guess, about two by three inches—bigger than a passport photo, with a checkered jacket on. I think it's one that was shown to me also—just a larger version of it was shown to me one day by a TV journalist in the programme. And he then sent one of his black juniors with us to go and show us Mr Mxenge's place of work, his motor car, which was parked opposite the offices, where there was at the time no building but just a prefab wall, and . . . the Audi which was parked behind the wall opposite Mr Mxenge's office. He then also went with us to show Mr Mxenge's house, and the information was also given to us that he usually works late at night, and his wife usually leaves before him. . . . According to my recollection, Sergeant Schutte brought Joe Mamasela [a black member of the Vlakplaas police operation] down on the 17th of November. . . . The next day some of the dogs got killed, I don't know exactly how many, and the idea was to leave it open for them to decide where they want to commit the murder, either at his place of work coming out, or on the road, or, if the situation might fall into their discretion as the right moment, at his house without being hampered by the dogs. Almond [Nofomela, another black member of the Vlakplaas security police] and Joe observed Mr Mxenge's office and his movements. The murder took place a day or two, if not three, after the poisoning of the dogs, and in fact on the night of the 19th of November. I had an arrangement with them that I would meet them. . . .

On the Thursday night of the 19th it was a rainy night. I did not do my usually early rendezvous of 8 and 9 o'clock, but did go there at 10 o'clock. I found the bakkie [pickup truck] with which they travelled parked in front of the pub in Field Street. I parked behind it and I went into the pub, where I found Joe Mamasela with Mr Mxenge's jacket on, his watch on his wrist. He handed me a wallet, which he said they took from Mr Mxenge, and car keys. They told me that they have already changed into new clothes, and I took all their old clothes and shoes from them, because the instructions was that they should dress in old clothes before the operation, and make sure that there is nothing in their pockets that could fall out or be left at the scene which could identify or may leave leads at the scene.... We arrived back at headquarters, and on Monday morning when I reported for work Brigadier Skoon's only question was concern again, "Have you left any possible traces or evidence at the scene," without discussing anything that had happened. At a stage—I can't remember whether it was during that same day—Brigadier Jan du Preez walked in and suggested that bounty money of R1 000,00 [1,000 rand] be paid to everyone involved. After asking a report from me, just in short what happened, with other words who did the killing and who not, I said the only people that was reported to me that did the stabbing of Mr Mxenge was Joe Mamasela, Almond Nofomela and David Tshikalanga. Brian Ngulungwa had just stood by with a gun, but never did any stabbing. The authorities then, Brigadier Jan du Preez and Brigadier Skoon, decided that only the three of them, namely Joe Mamasela, David Tshikalanga and Nofomela, the three of them would receive R1 000,00 each. Brian Ngulungwa did not receive any money. I shortly afterwards received R3 000,00 [3,000 rand] in cash, which I did not sign for . . . and handed the R1 000,00 then to the individuals that were involved.

33

Testimony of a Desertion

1997

From 1967 to 1991, all white South African men were conscripted into the South African Defence Force (SADF). Their service to the maintenance of white supremacy was sometimes embraced and sometimes grudgingly performed. Few openly resisted it. Beginning in the 1980s, however, some white conscripts rejected their conscription into the apartheid army, a few of them became conscientious objectors, and others fled the army itself. In this testimony to the TRC, a white conscript describes

Testimony of Mr. Ledgerwood, Truth and Reconciliation Commission, Special Hearing on Conscription, Cape Town, July 23, 1997, www.justice.gov.za/trc/special/conscrip /conscr02.htm.

the consequences of his desertion, which was a result of his growing political awareness.

The society that I grew up in had no questions about military duty, this was in 1980. You went to school[,] you registered when you were sixteen, you went off and did your National Service, you came home and life carried on as normal. Your girlfriend was proud to have somebody who was on the border [the border of Angola and Namibia] and the war was far, far away. None of us had ever been to Namibia.

. . . I tried to fit in like everybody does and to be the best that I could be but it didn't work because no matter what you did you were in trouble. The aim of basic training, which I understand now has changed was not to equip you with battle skills but was to break you down so that you would blindly follow orders and to provide recruits even in 1980, was some moral justification for being on the border. Every Wednesday morning after tea at ten o'clock we went to listen to the Dominee [a clergyman from the Dutch Reform Church] telling us why communism was such a bad idea. A few days later or a few lessons later socialism turned out to be a pretty bad idea too and after that it was a simple and short step to showing that democracy actually wasn't the best way you could run things and how America and Russia were actually on the same side. This was all based on the Bible. Here I was on much better ground because I knew my Bible better than the Dominee did and took pleasure in arguing with him until I was banned from the propaganda classes. . . .

One of the conclusions that I increasingly came to during my second year was that it was morally wrong, intrinsically wrong, evil in itself. There was no way that I could justify being involved in any way with the defence force. Although I had not and would not participate in any actions the whole atmosphere reeked of moral turpitude and all I had to go on was what the defence force told me. I thought then that believing what the SADF had to say about the ANC . . . was a bit like asking the devil for a reference on the Pope.

Eventually, in October it all came together. I got drunk one evening with some friends and we decided to go AWOL. . . . I'd hoped to be put into contact with the ANC to join Umkhonto we Sizwe and to work for something that I could at least believe in more than what I was involved in at that stage. It wasn't really that I supported the ANC[—]after all I didn't really know anything about them[—]it was just that I could not support the SADF. . . .

. . . Being young, foolish, unprepared and on my own I was caught. . . .
It was then that the nightmare began. I was handed over to . . . the security police who interrogated me for about two weeks or so. I can remember very few details except the screaming. I was nineteen years old at the
time. The dark nights of my soul had begun. . . . I can remember being
marched naked with a police blanket over me and handcuffed down the
main street . . . to the Magistrate's office where this kindly old gentleman
offered me some coffee and read my confession with growing horror.
The security police for example had insisted that I include the fact that
I was prepared to kill my own parents in the name of the struggle while
he carefully signed every page until the story was over. I think that the
absolute worst moment, worse even than the repeated interrogations
was the moment at Waterkloof Air Force Base when the security policeman escorting me back to Walvis Bay [South African base in Namibia]
took out his trip authorization to show the controller. He also showed a
body receipt for me which was all I was, a body, one body in transit to
Walvis Bay. One more dead body didn't matter. This was the same security policeman who'd just bought me a packet of cigarettes. . . .

. . . I was then handed over to Walvis Bay Security Branch where interrogation and torture continued. They thought that I was part of some
larger communist plot and the South West Africa Army Intelligence also
interrogated me. It was a relief to be handed over to military custody
after about two months. The military treated me far better than the police
did although the police came and fetched me from the military cells
every night for further interrogation. There were other incidents that I
can remember while in detention. Joking with the Colonel in charge of
Military Intelligence after being interrogated. Betraying everybody who
had ever said anything at all to me while I was under interrogation. The
shame at having been broken. A police Major telling me that he could
kill me and that no-one would know. And I think the most poignant of all,
being taken out to the spit of land outside of Walvis Bay Harbour the last
night of the interrogation and being given a cheese burger, chips and
a coke[,] having a smoke afterwards and the question, the same one I
would hear time and time again over the years, do you really think the
Blacks will ever govern this country?

34

Testimony of a Counterinsurgency Operation
1997

At a special hearing of the TRC, a white member of the South African Defence Force (SADF) unit Koevoet (the crowbar) described the unit's operations in Namibia and Angola. These operations targeted people fighting for Namibian liberation from South African colonialism and apartheid, specifically the South West Africa People's Organization (SWAPO). Beginning in 1967, all white South African men were conscripted into the army, but those involved in Koevoet volunteered for this supposedly elite military unit composed of mostly white officers and black soldiers. Their tactics were particularly brutal.

During this time . . . when I returned to Oshakati [SADF base of operations in northern Namibia] as a permanent member, we'd been out drinking one night and we went to visit some colleagues at our offices who were doing interrogations and these interrogations had been going on for a week non-stop around the clock. . . .

. . . We were crowded into a particular office where a school teacher was being interrogated[;] a huge explosive blast rocked the office and the lights flickered and went out. More blasts followed and it is obvious that we were under rocket attack. One of my colleagues shouted at the prisoner "kyk wat maak jou vriende," see what your friends are doing to us, and then started punching and kicking him and we all spontaneously joined in, including myself, we started kicking and assaulting this person this prisoner, we all spontaneously joined in.

The next day I was approached by a senior officer who said to me "julle het gisteraand kak gemaak," last night you really made shit didn't you? And when I asked why he replied that he and a second officer had been called out early that morning to dispose of the body of the prisoner that we had assaulted as he had died during the night. I was scared and I realised that I was a murderer now, but the official lack of response to the incident made me realise that this had happened before.

Testimony of Mr. Deegan, Ex–Koevoet Member, Truth and Reconciliation Commission, Special Hearing on Conscription, Cape Town, July 23, 1997, www.justice.gov.za/trc/special /conscrip/conscr03.htm.

So I killed somebody and there was no going back after that, I was one of them[;] I was part of the culture. . . . I was involved in torturing people, interrogating them using various methods but I never used methods like electric shocks or anything like that. I would approach it in a little more psychological level and try and win the person's confidence or trust, the old good cop bad cop routine and I was the good cop except sometimes things would get out of hand and I would respond angrily and start getting physical and actually assaulting prisoners. . . .

. . . On one occasion after capturing an insurgent we began to track his companion whose name was Congo. He was a well known political commissar and after tracking him for some time his tracks went to this kraal [village compound] and they didn't come out. I knew that he was inside this kraal complex and I was in charge of this team at the time as my team leader was away on leave. The tracks went in, the tracks didn't come out so it was obvious he was inside. The owner of the kraal, a very old man with white hair and thick glasses, I remember him very well and his family and small children, grandchildren were there and I asked this old man which hut this SWAPO guerrilla was in and he obviously didn't want to say because the local population, as in any war were just caught right up in the middle, they got it from both sides. They got it from SWAPO and they got it from us. If they didn't give information to either side they were just treated in the worst possible way so he didn't want to say anything so I gave an instruction to flatten a whole lot [of] huts. There were no people in these huts but these Casspirs [large armored vehicles] drove over the huts and he started getting really edgy and moving towards this hut and away from it and towards and away and then we identified that possibly this was the hut where this Congo, this political commissar was hiding out.

I gave the instruction for them to flatten the hut with the Casspir and that we would open fire at the same time. It's an overkill situation that was typically Koevoet. We would shoot as much concentrated fire into a space as possible, we didn't know how many people might be in there with him or what they were armed with and so on, so it was overkill just in case.

As we opened up[,] this rifle barrel of the person next to me was shot by the person next to him so the rifle barrel actually became bent and useless. He was firing an automatic and his gun blew up and it sounded like a hand grenade and what went through my mind was that this person in the hut had thrown this hand grenade at us. We were sprayed with shrapnel from the barrel of this gun blowing up and obviously this loud bang that went with it gave me such a shock that I ripped off the stock, I had an AK47, and I just kept firing, my hand was being burnt by the barrel but I was just crazy at that time and we were all firing.

Eventually we ceased fire and took the roof off this hut and there this man was lying very badly wounded. Our medic Shaun started putting a drip in him and patching him and trying to save his life and that's when I lost it completely, and I remember but I don't remember actually doing it but from accounts, from people actually telling me afterwards and from what I remember it was almost like an outer body experience where I could see myself after this had happened. There was a whole team standing there and I could see myself with a gun in my hand but what I actually did was I took out a gun and 9mm parabellum and I was interrogating this man and he wouldn't respond. He was badly wounded and he was going into unconsciousness and I just remember feeling the most incredible rage and anger that he was ignoring me and that he was lying at the time because he said "kandi shishi," he doesn't know anything. Then I brought the person that we'd captured the day before, they'd been travelling together and I said look here's your companion, we know your name is Congo[,] we know everything about you[,] the game's up, you're wounded[,] let's get this over with[,] tell us where your gun is, tell us where your rendezvous point is and then it's over. And he still denied it and I took out my pistol in a rage and put a bullet between his eyes, I shot him—I executed him.

After that it was as if I was looking at the scene from above and I could see myself standing there with this gun in my hand and everyone looking a bit shocked and the family from the kraal standing there and they were also very, very shocked and the kids were just very shocked. I walked away and I just said to the team clean up and I said to the owner of this kraal you must bury this body now[,] it's your responsibility, this is your problem and went back and I radioed in to our Commanding Officer who was in the radio room at the time and I said to him I want to come in because actually on the way to the vehicle I decided this is it. I've seen myself from another perspective, really like an aerial view of myself and I just couldn't believe who I was at the time, and I'd had enough[,] I wanted to come in, and he said follow up on your capture's information and I'll see you on Wednesday. This was a Sunday morning.

35

Testimony of an ANC Cadre and Captive

1997

In this selection, a young student from Cape Town describes how he left the country to join Umkhonto we Sizwe (MK) but found himself in various ANC detention camps in Angola under suspicion of being an enemy agent. These ANC camps held suspected spies and those who had disagreed with—and in some cases violently rebelled against—the MK hierarchy. Ntoni recounts the torture he experienced in the most notorious of these camps, Quatro. Such treatment was not as widespread as the generalized brutality of apartheid political repression. Nevertheless, his testimony reveals the violence found within ANC military structures, as well as the callousness with which schoolchildren were recruited, manipulated, and treated.

MR NTONI: I was recruited in 1980 at the time of the boycotts. I was [sixteen years old]. . . . An activist . . . came to me when I was with someone else who was active in the SRC [Students' Representative Council] at the school and told us that he was going to recruit people and if anyone wanted to go into exile he would assist that person. We agreed. . . .

MS GOBODO-MADIKIZELA: Before you left South Africa what would you say motivated you to leave and go to Lesotho?

MR NTONI: At that time we were involved in school activities. We were not politically aware yet. We knew that we were oppressed . . . but we continued to attend school until a sign came and we were told to come out of our closets and go and listen to somebody address us at a meeting and I think [it] was the fortnight before we wrote our June exam. So we went and listened and we realised that there were people that knew what was going on and perhaps they were people involved . . . in the ANC. At the time we just heard about the ANC, we did not know what it was all about. So what happened is that we became interested and decided that, in any way, these boycotts are going to continue. . . . We could see that parents were taking their children away and sending

Testimony of Anthony Thozamile Ntoni, Truth and Reconciliation Commission, Youth Hearings, May 22, 1997, www.justice.gov.za/trc/special/children/ntoni.htm.

them off to boarding schools because of the boycotts and so forth. So we realised that we should rather go into exile instead of sitting at home and doing nothing with all these boycotts. . . .

MS GOBODO-MADIKIZELA: Where were your parents at the time?

MR NTONI: They were there, but we did not involve them in what we were doing, because the people recruiting us told us that for our own safety it was best that we did not go round telling people what had happened, because they felt that even if our parents were to find out that we intended leaving the country they would panic and lots of people would get hurt.

MS GOBODO-MADIKIZELA: Your story begins when you arrived in Angola. If you could just tell us in your own words, when you left South Africa, where you went. Just tell us in a very coherent way, we went from there, how long you stayed there and where your rights were violated. Could you just start and tell us.

MR NTONI: I left South Africa in March 1981. We went straight to Lesotho. We stayed there for about a year and I left Lesotho in December, late in December. . . . We went to Mozambique. In Mozambique it was evident that we would not be able to pass through at the same time, because they needed so many people to celebrate January the eighth which I think was the ANC's birthday. We then performed there.

MS GOBODO-MADIKIZELA: What did you perform?

MR NTONI: We performed in cultural groups to celebrate the birthday of the ANC. After the January eighth celebrations we moved on to Angola. In Angola things, lots of things started to happen and we had arrived at night, late at night to, possibly, early in the morning at approximately three a.m. while many people were still sleeping.

MS GOBODO-MADIKIZELA: You got to Angola, in which camp did you arrive?

MR NTONI: We got to Viana Camp in Angola and that was at night and we were briefed there. We briefed them that we come from the other place and we were now at Viana Camp and we were going to look for people who were going to take part in the training.

MS GOBODO-MADIKIZELA: So it was basically a halfway station and selection point as such?

MR NTONI: Yes and there we were told that in Viana there were many South Africans [who] were possibly sent as spies from South Africa. If you saw anyone that you recognised there you should go and try and extract information from that person about the circumstances. What happened to me the first morning when I got up is that I saw a friend of mine from Langa [a township near Cape Town] and he and I had left the country in the same year.

When I saw him there in the morning I saw him sitting there and I went to him and said, hey, Mac what is happening and I saw that he was not too well. I knew him as someone that was very fit and healthy and who had been gymming and I wanted to know from him why he was so thin and sickly. He said, no, I have been arrested here. . . . Mac told me that this ANC representative in Zimbabwe, Joe Gqabi, had been shot and that he was implicated in the assassination. They were also accused of killing other people. So I was surprised when I heard that Mac had also been arrested and he was told to sign a statement admitting that he was involved in the murder of Joe Gqabi. So I wanted to know how was that possible, because Mac and I had left South Africa three months apart. . . . So I said, look, let us go to the Security Department [of the ANC] . . . and clarify this matter, because he said to me that he had been there for six months. . . . So I went to the Security Department and said, look, there is a certain person that you have got incarcerated here. I know him and if there is anything, any clarity you want on him, Mac is not involved in politics and he is not involved in these things. . . . They did not want to listen to me and dismissed me saying to me that I should leave and never speak to Mac again. That was the last time I saw Mac at the Viana Camp. . . . I also eventually left Viana Camp. . . .

I think after two or three months people came from the Viana Camp. It was another group who we were trained with. They came there before we could start training saying that Mac had been bitten by a snake and killed. . . .

We were at Caculama Camp. . . . I said how is that possible, then they said, no, Mac had been bitten and he fell and when they tried to wake him up he was not waking up and he was foaming at the mouth and his eyes were upturned and I asked them what kind of snake it was. They said they did not see it and I asked them where did the snake bite him, where was the wound. They said they did not see any wound and I said how is that possible, there were 30 or more of you. How can you not know, did the person not scream when he was bitten by the snake and they said no. Somebody said to me, why do you not just keep quiet. . . .

. . . What annoyed me even worse about Mac's story is that I was hoping that at least at his funeral they will say why he was being held at Viana Camp. They said, at his funeral they said that he was a hero and he wanted to be a communist and there was nothing to say why he was held in Viana. It was just said that Mac was a hero and then he was buried, that he wanted to become a communist.

Ms Gobodo-Madikizela: How did this matter affect you since you were defending Mac? How did it affect you at Caculama or your stay at the camp?

Mr Ntoni: . . . As soon as I went to confront them lots of other things started happening. . . . I saw a firearm lying in the grass and I realised that it might have been left mistakenly by an instructor and I picked it up out of curiosity and looked at it. I remember the last having this gun in my hand looking at it and turning it round and then all the officers were around me, assaulting me and they grabbed this firearm and then I was taken to a medical point and I was injected and I was dumped at a guardhouse which was near the gate . . . and while lying there, every time I tried to speak it felt like my tongue was swollen and I could not speak. I could not even move my fingers, they were stiff and . . . I slept there from the morning until shortly after lunch without being able to move.

Late at night about sunset a chief [named] Afrika arrived at the security camp and spoke to these people and they put me behind in a Land Rover and I was taken to another place where food stocks were kept approximately seven kilometres from the camp. I stayed there. I must have been there for approximately a month, but I cannot tell you exactly how long it was, because most of the time I was assaulted, but I really cannot say how long I stayed there, because sometimes Afrika would come there and assault me at times as well and I would never know why I was being assaulted. I was not thinking anything, all that was in my mind was these people, I do not know what these people are doing. All I want to do is train and all I want to do is leave here and go back and train.

The person that kept bringing me my food would tell me, do not worry, you are going to go back to the camp and train and he would be friendly and we would do exercises, but when exercising he would go behind me and assault me and when I lost consciousness he would leave me alone. What I do remember very well is Afrika took out a firearm which was his pistol which was at his waist and asked me, do you know this? I said, no, but I know that it is a gun. He took it and said to me, shoot. I said to him, no, this place is enclosed, how can I shoot and I followed his instruction and then he took his firearm back and assaulted me and asked me whether I knew about any rapes and I said, who did I rape at the camps. He made me sit down and he kicked my feet with boots until my skin came off. When they came in there they would assault me so badly. I remember the times when they would be there and every time I would come, I would lose consciousness and I would regain consciousness and find myself alone.

Then I was shifted to this house which was seven kilometres from the camp. They came in a green Mercedes Benz truck and tied me under the back seats. . . .

They then came in this truck and I was put in the back. The truck left. On the way I would lose consciousness quite often and there was a rope around my neck which would choke me from time to time and they would throw water over me for me to regain consciousness and then we would carry on and I think the first stop was at Luanda. I was then put in a goods container. I cannot remember for how long and from there we went to the ANC jail at Quatro. I do not know when I arrived at Quatro. . . .

. . . All I can remember now is between May and the time I recovered, because I did recover fully, on the first of January 1983, this was seven months during which I do not know what happened, but . . . by the time I recovered after seven months my left arm was nonfunctional and I could not speak and I had scars all over, I could not stand and I could not walk and I remember that. I remember sitting in a corner not knowing where I was, not knowing who the people around me were and they would call me . . . Mad Joe. So I would be worried, because I wanted to know who was Mad Joe and I remember picking up a firearm and looking at it, but I was now worried whether I had shot at anyone and wondering if I was in jail and so forth.

As time went by I got better and better and I could walk as well. One day I was called to the administration block and I was asked do you know Afrika Nkwe and I said, yes, I know him and I was told to go back to my cell. I went and I sat in the cell and all this time I could not speak to anyone. I could not know where I was coming from, why I was there. I was just staying there not knowing anything. My name was Mad Joe at that time. Everybody had their own names there. They would take us from one cell to another cell. We were then separated from the people who were in that first cell. We met new people, the others would go out to work in the garden and I would stay inside. They would suffocate me sometimes, my face was swollen up. I could not go out and work with others. . . .

Ms Gobodo-Madikizela: Did they tell you why they were harassing you, why they were torturing you?

Mr Ntoni: No, nobody came to me and nobody told me anything.

6

Living with Apartheid: Class, Race, and Gender

36

MABEL PALMER AND LILY MOYA

Correspondence

1949

The correspondence between a fifteen-year-old schoolgirl, Lily Moya, and a liberal white educator, Mabel Palmer, demonstrates Moya's desire for education and opportunities. The excerpts from this correspondence begin with a letter from Palmer to the "Native Commissioner" outlining Moya's situation. The letter also indicates the web of paternalistic bureaucracy that controlled Africans' lives even in rural areas. Moya's intelligence and perseverance were never rewarded. Perhaps out of frustration, she suffered a psychotic episode and was incarcerated for twenty-five years, after which she remained heavily dependent on drugs and hardly able to articulate her life story.

Shula Marks, ed., *"Not Either an Experimental Doll": The Separate Worlds of Three South African Women* (Durban: Killie Campbell Africana Library, and Pietermaritzburg: University of Natal Press, 1987), 68–74, 77–78.

University of Natal, Durban
14th April, 1949

The Native Commissioner,
Umtata.

Dear Sir:

I am the Organizer of the Non-European classes of the University of Natal, and apparently I have achieved some amount of publicity among the Bantu people as one who is willing to help members of the Bantu race who are anxious to get an education.

I have had a series of very pathetic letters from a Lily Moya who gives her address as P.O. Box 30, Umtata. She represents herself as an orphan in charge of a guardian who is not interested in her, and is not prepared to help her in her desire for further education. I gather she is only about 15 or 16 years old. She enquires if I could admit her to the classes of the University of Natal, but she is much too young, and has not yet passed her matriculation examination, but the letters are very well expressed giving me the impression of a young thing straining at the leash with desire for some training to fit her to take part in the life outside a native location.

When I remember the many people who helped me in years gone by to get the education which has enabled me to lead what has on the whole been a happy and successful life, I feel that I cannot shut my ears to her appeal.

But on consulting Mr Selby Ngcobo, one of the Bantu Research Workers in the University of Natal, he advises me to write to you on the subject, first of all to find out if the girl's story corresponds to the facts, and secondly to advise me as to whether there is anything I can do to help her. I did think of asking her to come to Durban, putting her in the Girl's Hostel, helping her to get work, and then arranging for her to take classes at the M. L. Sultan Technical Institution, but I have learnt since that the Women's Hostel in Durban is by no means a well-managed place, and that it would be most unsuitable as a place of residence for an innocent young girl.

I have now been wondering whether it would be possible to get her into any of the good native secondary schools, such as Adams or Inanda, but I should have to ask help from my friends in collecting special funds for this, and it seems desirable that I should first have some corroboration of the girl's story. I should be very much obliged if you could find out if the facts are as she states them and whether she appears to be a girl of whom it would be worth while to spend a good deal of money in order that she might attain her aim. In England such a girl would almost certainly win a scholarship from a primary to a secondary school, and then go on to the University.

I should be infinitely obliged for your help in this matter.

I am,
Yours very truly,
Dr Mabel Palmer

Office of the Magistrate, Umtata
27th April 1949

Dr Mabel Palmer,
Organizer, Non-European Section,
University of Natal, Durban.

Dear Madam:
re: Lily Moya

With reference to your letter of the 14th instant—I wish to inform you that I have investigated the case of the above-named girl and found the facts to be mainly as stated by her. According to the principal of the St. John's College she failed her Senior Certificate last year having obtained no higher symbol than "G" in all the subjects.

She will be 16 years old in August next and I do not consider that she ought to be sent to a city like Durban or Pietermaritzburg. She lives with her aunt in the Tsolo district where her guardian, her late father's brother, also resides. He states that he cannot afford to put her to school, having a family of his own.

As Lily is still very young I suggested to her that she look for employment for the balance of 1949 and reapply at the beginning of 1950.

Yours obediently,
MAGISTRATE—UMTATA

The Welcome Home, Umtata
1/5/49

The Secretary,
The Non-European Section, N.U.C.,
Durban.

Dear Madam:

Yours latest received. Contents well notified and greatly encourageous. I've been called by the Native Commissioner here at Umtata. He has given me no better plan than yours. I must say it out, because he has forbidden me from leaving Umtata and said that the only plan he gives me is that I should find work here at Umtata and then apply earlier to St. John's College as a day scholar. I'm still too young to go to Durban, a very disagreeable place and I mustn't worry myself—there is still a long time in front of me.

On that day, 26th April, I also went to ask the St. John's Principal Teacher to admit me in as a day scholar student, he agreed but after talking this over with the Warden, the latter said that it is too full. I made a mistake by applying to the Principal Teacher at first. The Boarding master said that a case like mine occured last year with the same result. The Warden hates that the Principal Teacher should admit children without his consent at first, even if they have to be day scholars.

What I want to do is Corresponding this year if I can get some-one to pay for the tuition—at a session's period. I've posted two letters to two of these Corresponce [*sic*] Colleges, to choose the better from them. I have asked their tuition and if I could take the only subjects I've failed but sure to get an exemption in matric at the end of the year.

When you answer me also explain to me this and give me your real opinion on this. Don't be mislead to your consideration which you said you'll do in silence, by this letter. Tell me your decision when you write me.

Thanks I give to you for what you have promised to do for me, sending books, cannot be verbally described. Only Him who knows how thankful I am to you. When answered by the Secretary and Registrar of the Correspondence College I'll tell you what they say or enclose the letters in for you.

Books I'd like you to send me are "King Lear" (a play by Shakespeare) 2. "Jane Eyre" 3. "Admirable Chrichton." Can be glad if you give me too their summaries. I shall tell you the other books later, which I would like to read for pleasure.

You will not mind not answering me always. I confide in your advice and hope for your sincere consideration to all I write you.

Can be very glad if you correct my English errors and tell me when I'm getting worse or ameliorating.

With Greetings,

I am,
Yours truly,
Lily P. Moya

The Welcome Home, Umtata
20-5-49

The Secretary, The Non-European Section, N.U.C.,
Durban.

Dear Madam:

It disappoints me too severely when you don't reply me. I really don't know what to do now. I thought your answer to my letters would come earlier so that this time I would be busy with studies, I mean with reading the books.

Pardon me, if I've annoyed you in any case with my previous letter, to you. I also who ask you to correct my errors.

You said you would consider what to do about me, I hope then you've not forgotten your promise, and please after your conclusion write me I beg you.

It seems to me as if there is this person who always desuades you from helping me, if there is really any-one desuading you, please pay a deaf ear to that person's unphilanthropic advice.

The books I earnestly need are:

1. King Lear

2. Admirable Chrichton

3. Essays of To-Day

4. Queene Victoria

and 5. Living Tradition (Poems)

and 6. "Jane Eyre"

You may not worry yourself about "Jane Eyre" for the present moment I have finished reading it. I found it in the Native Public Library. Had it (Library) not been so narrow I would look for the rest of the books I need and read them.

I can be very glad if you can answer this letter of mine at your earliest possible. You may not say what you think to do for me if you haven't yet finished considering the matter. But, please send me the books.

Let me not expatiate,

With greetings, from
Yours sincerely,
Lily Moya

The Secretary,
The Welcome Home, Umtata.
14/6/49

The Secretary,
The Non-European Section, N.U.C.,
Durban.

Dear Madam:

I'm really stranded. You seem to have completely withdrawn from giving me any help. I am puzzled. I cannot tell whether you are still considering my state of affairs as your promise in your last letter or you have been completely desuaded by your advisers, against helping me.

There is no painful switch than the one you have threshed me with, not replying my letters. It is too difficult for me to guess, what causes you to suddenly change your mind against me.

Anyway—I don't fully claim you as my adviser, but, you have taught me to trust in you, in your last letter.

Promise me this, will you please take me in your school Adams College if I've struggled to pass the Senior Certificate Examination which may be a Cape or National Exemption one? It may-be next year or next year but one (1950 or 1951). Please I urgently ask for your reply to this particular note I write you.

All along I shall be expecting for yours, but please try, though you may be too busy and occupied, to give me an early reply, since I may perhaps be moving away in few weeks or days to seek work which may give me better earnings to help me to buy few articles such as clothing materials and so on.

Let me not expatiate.

So, Best greetings and love, from
Lily Patience Moya

University of Natal, Durban
17th June 1949

Miss L. P. Moya,
The Welcome Home, Umtata

Dear Miss Moya:

You really must not become so impatient if you do not hear from me immediately. I am a very busy woman with a great deal to do for my own students, and it is only because your first letter appealed to me that I was willing to interest myself in your case. When I learnt from the Native Commissioner that you were only 15 and had not done well in your Senior Certificate last year, I realised that he was quite right in saying that you should not leave Umtata, and that anything beyond sending you books of which I have copies myself, there is nothing I can, or ought, to do for you until next year. I will try to get some of the books to you as soon as possible, but I do not know what you mean by item 4—"Queen Victoria." There are a great many books about Queen Victoria and you must give me more details. Is it Lytton Strachey's Queen Victoria? King Lear and Jane Eyre I can send you immediately. I am only *lending* them, and will enclose little slips for you to sign and you must send these back to me at once, and return the books towards the end of the year. I may put in one or two other books that I think may interest you.

I certainly approve of your attitude that you should complete your matriculation or Senior Certificate by correspondence, though if you only got "G" in all the subjects, as I am informed by the Umtata Magistrate, you will need to work very hard. You need to be careful about the correspondence colleges, as some of them are very poor indeed, but the University Correspondence at Pretoria (though I am not sure that this one does pre-matriculation work) and the Rapid Results College in Mentieth House, Smith Street, Durban are both reliable. You might let me see them as soon as you have the answers from the correspondence colleges. I might, though I make no promises, be able to help you with the fees. For next year I have a plan for you in mind, but as I am not at all sure whether I shall be able to carry it out, I prefer to say nothing of it in the meantime.

I can only end by repeating what I have said before. I will not forget about you, but you must not expect me to arrange things in a hurry nor to answer your letters immediately. There are many people who have stronger claims on my attention and action than you yourself.

Yours sincerely,
(Dr) Mabel Palmer

37

NON-EUROPEAN AFFAIRS DEPARTMENT

Your Bantu Servant and You
1962

Since black labor was so central to white economic prosperity, the apartheid system, while segregating white and black, also placed them in close proximity. Most white households employed live-in black domestic servants. The state offered "expert" advice on the treatment of such servants: Boundaries between white women and black men needed to be policed, "tribal" customs respected, and tasks deemed too complex limited. State paternalistic ideology was complemented by the paternalism evident in the correspondence between Lily Moya and Mabel Palmer excerpted in Document 36.

Much of the tension which exists between the different racial groups in the country can be eased by you playing your part in giving serious attention to the human relationship factor in the handling of your Bantu domestic servant. Generally it can be said that where there is courtesy and mutual respect, between people of different groups, this permeates into the group as a whole. As an employer of Bantu, you can therefore help tremendously in establishing a harmonious relationship between the European and the Bantu of this country. Good Black/White relations very often have their foundation in the home, and the Golden Rule "Do unto others as you would have them do unto you" could result in mutual goodwill and respect. If all members of your household treat a servant with recognition of his dignity as a human being, he will respond and reciprocate.

Women should be exceptionally careful in the treatment of male servants. In tribal life a woman is always regarded as a minor and remains under the tutelage of a man. She must always act with due respect and modesty towards and in front of males. A women employer can enhance her reputation with her male servant by observing the following basic rules of behaviour in her dealings with him:—

    (i) Always behave towards him with the same dignity and modesty that you would behave towards a male of your own race. Above

Non-European Affairs Department, *Your Bantu Servant and You* (Johannesburg, 1962).

all, never appear in front of him in any state of undress, or allow any female in the family to so appear.

(ii) Do not leave girls in his care. It never happens in tribal society.

(iii) Do not expect him to make your bed, wash or iron your under-clothing or those of girls, nor to wash stained linen. It outrages his sense of what is proper.

(iv) Never give vent to annoyance in an undignified way and never allow children to speak to him in any other but dignified and courteous terms. Respect always breeds respect.

(v) Every person has a name dear to him, because in his own mind he identifies himself with his name. Therefore, never address your servant in any other way or by any other name but the one originally given to you as his name. "Boys," "Jim" (or "Mary" to females) as a form of address gives much more offence than is generally realised.

Although many Bantu have been born and educated in European areas and could, therefore, with some justification, be regarded as westernized to a degree, the majority of male domestic servants are still tribalised to a greater or lesser extent with limited knowledge of the European way of life. Many of them have also a very limited understanding of any other language but their own. To obviate any misunderstandings and possible annoyances, it is desirable that you:—

(a) Use the language he understands reasonably well when giving instructions. You will create good will towards yourself and your family if you are able to speak his language, failing which a related Bantu language, or in the last resort some form of lingua franca such as "fanagalo." Inexpensive booklets on "fana-galo" are available at all booksellers.

(b) Give instructions clearly and concisely. Be positive. Say "Do this," not "Don't do that."

(c) Make sure that he understands what is required of him. He thinks it polite to say "Yes" even if he did not understand what you said.

(d) Give orders one at a time. Very few servants are able to follow, remember and carry out a series of instructions in the correct order, or at all, for that matter.

(e) Try to organise the work into a proper routine and interrupt the routine as little as possible. Do not call him from routine work to do another task.

(f) Show him everything that he has to do within the shortest possible period after employment. Gradual introduction of new tasks, is seen as an innovation of duties he was not originally employed to perform.

38

BRAM FISCHER

Speech from the Dock

1966

An Afrikaner from a prominent family, Bram Fischer served as Nelson Mandela's lawyer during the Rivonia Trial before he joined the South African Communist Party (SACP). In this extract from his trial for attempting to overthrow the government, Fischer describes the emergence of his racial consciousness as a white Afrikaner and his realization of its irrational basis. Fischer was imprisoned until shortly before his death from cancer in 1975.

Though nearly forty years have passed, I can remember vividly the experience which brought home to me exactly what this "White" attitude is and also how artificial and unreal it is. Like many young Afrikaners I grew up on a farm. Between the ages of eight and twelve my daily companions were two young Africans of my own age. I can still remember their names. For four years we were, when I was not at school, always in each other's company. We roamed the farm together, we hunted and played together, we modeled clay oxen and swam. And never can I remember that the colour of our skins affected our fun or our quarrels or our close friendship in any way.

Then my family moved to town and I moved back to the normal White South African mode of life where the only relationship with Africans was that of master to servant. I finished my schooling and went to University. There one of my first interests became a study of the theory of segrega-

"Speech from the Dock by Bram Fischer, March 28, 1966 (abridged)," in Thomas G. Karis and Gail M. Gerhart, *From Protest to Challenge: A Documentary History of African Politics in South Africa, 1882–1990*, vol. 5, *Nadir and Resurgence, 1964–1979* (Bloomington: Indiana University Press, 1997), 367–68.

tion, then beginning to blossom. This seems to me to provide the solution to South Africa's problems and I became an earnest believer in it. A year later, to help in a small way to put this theory into practice, because I do not believe that theory and practice can or should be separated, I joined the Bloemfontein Joint Council of Europeans and Africans, a body devoted largely to trying to induce various authorities to provide proper (and separate) amenities for Africans. I arrived for my first meeting with other newcomers. I found myself being introduced to leading members of the African community. I found it hard to shake hands with them. This, I found, required an enormous effort of will on my part. Could I really, as a White adult, touch the hand of a Black man in friendship?

That night I spent many hours in thought trying to account for my strange revulsion when I remembered that I had never had any such feelings towards my boyhood friends. What became abundantly clear was that it was I and not the Black man who had changed, that despite my growing interest in him, I had developed an antagonism for which I could find no rational basis whatsoever. . . .

. . . I came to understand that colour prejudice was a wholly irrational phenomenon and that true human friendship could extend across the colour bar once the initial prejudice was overcome. And I think that was lesson No. 1 on my way to the Communist Party, which has always refused to accept any colour bar and has always stood firm on the belief, itself two thousand years old, of the eventual brotherhood of all men.

39

MBUYISENI OSWALD MTSHALI

Amagoduka at Glencoe Station

1971

In this excerpt of a renowned poem, Mbuyiseni Oswald Mtshali describes the songs of a group of migrant workers (the amagoduka, *those who come and go) as they wait at a station to catch a train that will take them from their rural homes to the gold mines. It evokes their exploitation, the danger of the work, the masculine working culture, the impoverishment of rural*

Mbuyiseni Oswald Mtshali, *Sounds of a Cowhide Drum* (Johannesburg: Renoster Books, 1971; reprint, Johannesburg: Jacana Media, 2012), 164–68.

lands, homes and families, even while shaming those who do not go to work on the mines (the loafers).

The two began to sing,
their voices crying for the mountains
and hills of Msinga, stripped naked of
their green garment.

They crossed rivers and streams,
gouged dry by the sun's rays,
where lowing cattle genuflected
for a blade of grass and a drop of water
on a riverbed littered with carcasses and bones.

They spoke of hollow-cheeked maidens
heaving drums and brackish water
from a faraway fountain.

They told of big-bellied babies
sucking festering fingers
instead of their mother's shriveled breasts.

Two cockroaches
as big as my overcoat buttons
jived across the floor
snatched meat and bread crumbs
and scurried back to their hideout.

The whole group joined in unison:
curious eyes peered through the frosted windows
"*Ekhaya bafowethu!* Home brothers!"

We come from across the Tugela River;
We're going to the Golden City! Golden City!
where they will turn us into moles
that eat the gold dust
and spit out blood.

We'll live in compounds
where young men are pampered
into partners for older men.

We'll visit shebeens
where a whore waits for a fee

to leave your balls burning
with syphilitic fire.

If the black gods of our ancestors
are with us
we'll return home
to find our wives
carrying babies known
only to themselves and loafers.

40

JÜRGEN SCHADERBERG

The Destruction of Sophiatown
1955, 1959

In the first photograph of this selection, Jürgen Schaderberg, a photographer for the popular Drum *magazine, illustrates the determined resistance of the residents of Sophiatown, one of the last racially mixed communities near the center of Johannesburg. The second photograph, taken four years later, depicts the ultimate destruction of Sophiatown. In its place, the white suburb termed* Triomf *[Triumph] was built. Such forced removals aimed to eradicate the emergent black and multiracial urban way of life.*

Jürgen Schaderberg/Getty Images.

Jürgen Schaderberg/Getty Images.

41

GAJIDA JACOBS

Forced Removals in Cape Town

1990

In this interview, part of an oral history project to collect the memories of those forced out of Cape Town, Mrs. Gajida Jacobs, a coloured woman who lived in District Six, recalls her childhood prior to forced removals. She describes the consequences of the proclamation of separate amenities and the Group Areas Act (1950), including the relocation of people from District Six, near the center of Cape Town, to Cape Flats settlements such as Manenberg on its outskirts. The effect of forced removals on her previous sense of community is striking.

Interview with Mrs. Gajida Jacobs, Centre for Popular Memory, University of Cape Town, June 3, 1990. Abridged. Source: © Centre for Popular Memory, University of Cape Town, 2008.

[INTERVIEWER]: *Did you ever go for walks, or go fishing?*

[JACOBS]: Me and my Auntie used to go walk to the Gardens—always when it was nice weather, then me and my aunt and my uncle and the old lady next door and her children[,] she had about three, we would all take a walk down to the Gardens. Those were happy days. They were nice times. That time the European people. Coloured people. Black people all mixed. There was no argument about . . . "You can't sit here. You can't sit there" on the benches you know. . . . Then afterwards they marked all that, this is for Europeans, this is for Coloureds. They even marked the benches; [even] on the Station. I know, I can remember one day I went to the Station, I was quite a big girl[,] 15 or 16, or so and I just want to sit down. I was tired. There was me and another girl and we just sat down, flopped down on the bench and, God, those people, the railway police. It wasn't Coloureds then, it was all boere [Boers]. GET UP, blady Hotnots [Hottentot, a derogatory term for coloureds], look where you sit. STAAN OP STAAN OP! [STAND UP! STAND UP!] And I got such a fright, you know I'm laughing now but I got such a fright and the other girl, that I just ran. . . . See we didn't know that time apartheid was in. We children didn't know what apartheid means—see it was first segregation—before apartheid. Apartheid segregation was one word. Then when all this came in. They made it Apartheid! But it was really segregation—an English word; [so] it didn't sound so harsh! And many of us didn't know what segregation meant but Apartheid—we just got to know that. "Hey—weet jy – watch waarom jou sit!" [Hey—Do you know—Watch where you sit!] He said it like that. Man and there the train came in and it was full—, full of European people, and I felt so embarrassed. I knew, I felt so ashamed—so I just run, I was frightened, I was scared. Afterwards, I was angry when I was home and so, and I tell my Uncle about it, but when it happened. At that moment, I just felt so ashamed. It sort of came over me that I've done something wrong, and all the people was looking at me; I felt guilty for doing nothing—just for sitting on a bench. . . .

I: *Was politics discussed in the house?*

J: Yes it was discussed but it was not for us children. It was for big people. Like today, you can't discuss everything with everybody—like politics. You don't know who squeals and then you go to gaol. But in those days people didn't go to gaol. No man, the gaol was empty at that time. . . .

I was also a bit interested afterwards but I was afraid. Afraid to speak out. But I got cross, man. I got cross in my heart. But that was only after the Nationalists came in. Before it was never like that. We felt equal like. We didn't earn a lot of money, but the White people was different. They were like people that were sorry for us. You come with a hard story to them, the Madam or the Master would give you; they would never chase you away. Today, you go to their places, they call for the police. . . .

I: *What do you feel about the Group Areas Act that moved you from town?*
J: Oo, don't talk about that, please don't talk about it to me. I will cry. I will cry all over again. There's when the trouble started. When they chuck us out like that. When they chucked us out of Cape Town. My whole life came changed! There was a change. Not just in me, in all the people. What they took away they can never give it back to us! Even if they give it back we won't take it. It won't ever be the same again. (Weeping) It cannot be the same. The trust we had in those people, and they broke their trust. (Weeping . . .) Oh I want to cry so much, all over again—when I talk about it. . . . I cannot explain how it was when I moved out of Cape Town and I came to Manenberg. It took me a couple of years to get used to it—until I could think I must just be satisfied. In those days I didn't know why they chuck us out. I didn't know. What was wrong? Why they chuck us out—what did we do! Those questions I asked myself over and over. What did we do that they chuck us out like this? We wasn't murderers, we wasn't robbers like today. Now people are corrupt! Ever since they put us in these places, our boys, our children can become corrupt. They can be really barbarians! Skollies [hoodlums] and barbarians. They murder one another and that is what they wanted. They wanted us to fight one another and that way we can get less. Afterwards I realised all this. It was wrong—I know it was wrong what the White people did. Those people did us wrong. If we were in their shoes we would never have done that! They had everything, everything that a person's heart yearns for. And we had nothing, but we were satisfied. They broke us up. They broke communities up. The happiness they took from us. They took our happiness from us! (Weeping.) . . . .

I: *But now you don't feel good about our rulers?*
J: No man! But I don't want to speak about politics. But the day they threw us out of Cape Town. Oo my God that was my whole life tumbling down! I don't know how my life continued. I couldn't see my life in this raw township! You know, far away from family. All the neighbours were strangers. That was the hardest part of my life, believe

me. I came out of my door and I was looking into [strangers'] places. It took us time to get accustomed to one another. We had to find out all about each other—they really destroyed us when they did this thing. They destroyed us; they made our children ruffians. . . . My son hired a video and he brought this film [about] the Bronx. . . . I can remember the Bronx had buildings like this, I think [it's] in America. And I looked that night, we saw the film but you know what I reckon when I came to bed—I think it's like us. Just like us, living in tenement buildings. Little buildings, shapeless, just like us living here. It's every day the same—looking out your window.

42

Interview with a Member of the Matoks Community

1979

By the 1970s, with the full-fledged application of separate development, wide-ranging forced removals of Africans from disputed rural and peri-urban areas to homelands occurred. Many of these forced removals attracted little attention from major political groups, in part because they concerned marginal, poor, and semiliterate rural people. In this interview, a community member describes how the apartheid state tried to ensure that people agreed to the removal process by co-opting local elites, including chiefs, magistrates, and lawyers. In this case, however, a carefully orchestrated community campaign managed to prevent forced removals.

You should know that the tribal authority members are being paid by the magistrate. So when they need to remove people they start with members of the tribal authorities. They talk to them, take them to the place where they will be moved to. They also take the chief. Show him around. Show him the house that he will live in. In many cases this is the

"Matoks Location, Bandelierkop: Interview with a Member of the Community," in Laurine Platzky and Cherryl Walker, *The Surplus People: Forced Removals in South Africa* (Johannesburg: Ravan Press, 1985), 250–54.

house of a white man and he gets taken inside. Officials get promised a bonus if they persuade the people to be moved to the place.

As soon as this thing started we knew that the tribal authorities are on good terms with the magistrate and we formed an executive committee not from tribal authorities alone, but also people who were against the removal and people who could reason well, level-headed. We did not want people interested in riots; that's what we want to avoid. Then from this we built up a committee and the first thing we did was to convince the chief that we think the removals are no good. We showed him all the things: took him around; make him aware of the fact that he is the chief of all these people who will get nothing, and who are aware that he will get any car that he asks for from them. Then we invited him to a meeting. We address the meeting on his behalf and get him to say: "What my people say, is what I endorse." So when these people came to address us he told them: "What the people say, is what I endorse." He said this to the commissioner and told him how long we've been here and that we are not being paid for being put in the streets like this. And so the donkeys were taken away "free of charge." We were not paid. Then we said, "Now look, we are leaving our forefathers' graves here and what we saw happening in the past we wouldn't like to see happening again. The farmers who will take this place, the first thing that they do is plough over these graves."

The committee must always talk in front of the chief. If you hold any meeting in the absence of the chief, you are not covered. If he's there, then never mind. So in his presence we drew up a memorandum of the reasons why we think we should not go. We happened to know the place where they wanted to move us to. We went there, using our own transport and looked at the place. We saw what advantages and what disadvantages it had. Then we were able to compile a good memorandum comparing the two places. We were to be moved to Kromhoek and Eindermaak, a very dry, hot and rocky place. We travelled around all these places. We were lucky to get a map from some of the clerks at the Magistrate's office.

When we were through with the chief commissioner we asked them to call someone who is senior to him. So they called Mr Serfontein who is the secretary. He's the man who's busy with removals. So he came and we talked to him and wrote down all that was said. You see you have to choose all the speakers and have to draft what they have to say. They've got to subtract nor add nothing from their speech. We gave him a copy of all the speeches. We told him that we feel we have to take this to the Minister of Cooperation and Development. So he took the copies.

And then later we requested a meeting with him [the Minister] and then we wrote to Phatudi [Chief Minister of Lebowa] also that he also should be present. So after six months or so he agreed and came. . . . We had now a polished memorandum.

We told them we're not interested in riots. There's not a single person who's going to throw a stone at you. All we are interested in is that we retain our place. You people (the Government) said that you can solve anything by way of consultation. We said, now we are here on consultation and if you say you are not forcing anything we are saying that we are not prepared to move. We want to tell you straight away, our chiefs too, they endorse all what we've said. We drove them around, showed them all the places, showed them all what we had done and all the schools and the new school blocks just constructed.

We wouldn't like to destroy these things, because we have to remember the names of certain people.

We tell them we know that you can build good schools where you want us to go, but we feel we must stay here.

You see, if you get a lawyer you are sure to go away. Because these lawyers . . . when they come they tell you: "Look, this is a government regulation, it's passed in parliament. It is cut and dry. There's nothing you can do to it except move." So we said, "Now we do away with lawyers and we handle our cases" — and we handled our cases ourselves. We paid nothing to the lawyers. So we faced the commissioner and the Ministers. We told them: "You've got all the weapons, everything, and you could force us to go, but we will not go. We will not fight back but we will not go." We will not go. This is the main thing. . . .

These lawyers from Legal Resources only want us to get better compensation. So we said: "We don't want anybody here who will get us better compensation. We don't want to go. As soon as we start discussing this question of compensation then they start numbering houses. The question of compensation must be completely cut out."

As soon as you start mentioning "compensation" they start numbering the houses. They suddenly arrive with buckets of paint. You confront them: "Before you write down anything you go to the chief's kraal for permission." They've been given instructions to avoid violence as far as possible. So they won't cause trouble if they are not allowed to paint the houses.

They also come to your house with a big iron bar and make holes in your walls and floors to see what they are made of. Then they add R5 [5 rand] here, R30 [30 rand] there and so on. Then they subtract the money you owe them for transport. And later you have to pay for the tents. So forget about compensation. . . .

When the officials come and ask questions, do not answer anything. You may think it is a good answer you are giving them, but you find out that it may have other implications. Tell him: "Give us time to think about these questions." Discuss them. Try and find out what the implications of the questions are and then work out a reply.

Consequently there has been no violence here. At Makgato district, there wouldn't have been any violence, but the commissioners won the support of the chief. So the chief signed for the removals. There it was different. He signs on behalf of the community. So the trucks come and everybody had to move. People refused and the police came and broke windows, took out all the people's possessions and then went into the bush to search for the owners. They used dogs and trucks to find the people. There was a lot of violence, mainly because the chief had agreed to move.

A lot of people came this way seeking refuge and when they came to look for them we refused to allow them in the village. We said: "If a man asks for cover we cannot say no. All we can do is talk to them and see how they feel about moving out."

All the time they stayed here and now they've moved back to Makgato once they heard of the reprieve given to the area by the government. The government is now drilling new boreholes [wells] and the people are now fixing their damaged houses.

We (the committee) have been intimidated a bit. They wanted to know what we discussed. We said that all our meetings are open. We don't hide what we discuss. We were asked if any outsiders, agitators, whites were involved. We said no. We are dealing with our problems ourselves.

We found out about the talk of our removals in 1975. The magistrate sent the chief a letter asking him to a meeting with the tribal authorities. We were tipped, however, that the meeting was to talk about resettlement. So instead of the tribal authority going to the meeting, the committee went. The magistrate objected about this and we replied that it is not only the tribal authority that will be moved but the people and we represent their interests and any decisions taken by the tribal authority will not be binding. . . .

What happens with the chiefs is that they either give them a house or a car or both. Sometimes they send them overseas to make press statements about how nice the place is. Meanwhile the people here starve. Once people have moved there they start asking the chief to pay back for the car he got from the government and so the chief starts taxing his people more.

43

EMMA MASHININI

Push Your Arse!

1989

Emma Mashinini, a South African trade unionist and anti-apartheid activist, describes her first factory job, including the tensions between work and family life, and the harsh conditions on the factory floor. Apartheid forced urban workers to live many miles away from their place of employment. Mashinini's memoir demonstrates the domestic and public arenas in which black women experienced discrimination and exploitation.

I remember my first day very clearly. It was November, and when I walked into that building it seemed to me that there were hundreds of people rushing this way and that, and a terrible volume of noise, with a lot of shouting—"Come on, do your job!"—that kind of thing. It was completely bewildering. Immediately I got there, on my first day as a worker, I was started on the machines, working very close to the people who had already worked as machinists at other factories, so I was a struggler from the start. I remember most of all how they cursed us when we couldn't keep up. I was in a department headed first by an Afrikaner called Mrs Smit and then by a German-speaking man, Mr Becker. He used to shout and scream at us, sometimes for no reason at all, and it wasn't unusual for ten people to be dismissed a day. They were always saying you had to push. They would say, "*Roer jou gat*," which means, "Push your arse"—"Come on, push your arse and be productive." You would be on the machine sweating, but they would tell you, "*Roer jou, Roer jou*"—"Push, push, push," and you would push and push. No one would ever say, "Okay, that's enough. Good." You were working for a target. You'd know there was a target you had to meet, and at the back of your mind you were concerned about the welfare of your children. You would be torn in two, because you were at work and in your mind you were at home. This is the problem of the working mother: you are divided. You are only working because you have to.

Emma Mashinini, "Push Your Arse!," in *Strikes Have Followed Me All My Life* (1989; repr., New York: Routledge, 1991), 14–16.

Penny was almost three when I moved to the central factory, and she'd started going to a crèche nearby, so I didn't have a baby that I had to carry from one place to another, because even though I stopped work much later than the crèche closed, and after my other two children came home from school, I had a neighbor who wasn't working and she looked after them. But still at work you were thinking of the children, and at home you were thinking of the job, and then you had this extra person to bother about—a husband.

I'd start factory work at seven-thirty in the morning, after travelling about thirty kilometres to get there. Other workers came from double that distance. . . . People would be sleeping on the trains. Some would have been travelling for a long time, and even before the train there would be some distance to go for a bus stop, and the bus would have already been travelling and picking up more people. So if you had to be at your machine at seven-thirty you would have to be at your work-place by seven, and you would have to be ready to take the train at five. For some it could be about four.

I would leave my children sleeping, and the night before I would have made my preparations for the coming day, because I had to leave everything—bread, uniform, everything—lined up for my neighbor, who would come and wake my children for school. There would be nothing for you at the factory—no tea, no coffee. The tea-break was at a certain time, and if you had brought something from home that would be when you would eat, in that ten-minute tea-break later in the day. And if you brought nothing, your tea-break would be exhausted while you were walking to the canteen and queuing there. By the time you got your coffee and sat down, five minutes had gone, and you would have to swallow everything and run to be back on time.

I would get home about seven—and in winter, you know, that was pretty dark. When I got home I'd start making a fire on my coal stove. I used to try to prepare for that the night before, but if not I would have to start chopping wood, getting the coal, getting the ashes out and all that. And there was no one to follow my children when they were getting up, and the basin would be full of dirty water, and I would start emptying that as well, picking up the dirty clothes, and the school clothes they took off when they got home from school, and all that before I actually started cooking.

My husband would not be rushing to come home. What would he rush to come home for? When he got out from his job he would go wherever he wanted to, and because he was a man it had to be so. I couldn't question him, or ask him, and anyway when he got home my time was interfered with because I had to have water to give him to wash his hands—not just ordinary cold water, but warm water. While my fire was still burning I would pump the primus stove [kerosene stove] quickly to get the warm water for my dear husband to wash his hands, and then with the remaining water I would make tea. I would also enjoy that, but standing, because my fire would be burning for me to cook our main meal. My husband would sit and read the newspaper—and sometimes I would wonder if he really understood what he read, or if he just knew that the white boss sits when he comes home, and reads his newspaper.

I never thought to compare. I never thought that while the white boss was doing that, sitting and reading, there was a black man or woman doing everything for them. It was just the order of the day that I had to do everything. And if, after he washed, he emptied the water instead of just leaving it standing, I would be so grateful. I would feel that was so nice of him.

44

Diary of a Thirteen-Year-Old Schoolgirl from Soweto

1982

Even while apartheid authorities attempted to limit migration to urban areas, large urban settlements emerged outside the main towns, in so-called townships, such as the South West Townships (Soweto) outside Johannesburg. By the 1980s, this urban community, in particular the youth, was enmeshed in quotidian violence even as residents attempted to pursue their education and construct a sense of community.

August 20, 1982 (Friday)

Left school at 3:25—caught a 4 o'clock bus—arrived at 5 p.m. at home— went to the shops to buy cold drink—on my way met a dirty boy— greeted me "thugsy like" but I did not answer him—he gave me a hot

"13-Year-Old Girl (R.M.)," in Mbuyiseni Oswald Mtshali, *Give Us a Break: Diaries of a Group of Soweto Children* (Johannesburg: Skotaville, 1988), 60–64.

clap [slap]—and I did not do anything but just looked at him—he realised I am not one of his type—the thing that amazes me the most is that they don't wash themselves but they expect us to fall in love with them—that is what I always ask myself—he went away and I went back home—watch TV—had a bath—ate my supper—went to bed at 11:30.

August 21, 1982 (Saturday)

Woke up early in the morning—ate my breakfast—went to the bus stop—where I met my boyfriend—who proposed to love me one month ago—but I didn't want to write anything about him in my diary—and there is no reason—we went to school—and he told me that he waited for me at the bus stop—because it was weekend so that he cannot lose me for I can see other boyfriends—returned home by 6 p.m.—while I was sitting home—my mother received a call—the one who phoned asked my mother if she mind for them to come and eat supper with us—my mother was frightened because nowadays people are incompletely reliable—we waited for them—only to find out that it was my boyfriend with his parents—we ate a nice supper—and they left at 10 p.m.—went to bed at 11:30.

August 22, 1982 (Sunday)

Woke up early in the morning—went to play tennis—on my way met somebody who was stabbed to death. . . . I wondered that how a murderer feels when he/she kills other people—went back home with joy—prepared my school uniform—ate my supper—went to bed at 9:00.

August 30, 1982 (Monday)

Left school at 3:25—caught a 4 p.m. bus—arrived at 5 p.m.—while I was undressing my school uniform telephone rang—it was my boyfriend's mother—she told me about my boyfriend's illness—I dropped the receiver, caught a taxi and went to see him—he was very glad to see me, and I was very glad too. He kissed me and wished me a pleasure "bye"—returned home at 6 p.m.—sat down and thought about many things—realise that you've got a boyfriend—must let your parents know about that, do not just go outside at night to see your boyfriend in the streets because murderers can kill you—beside murders the girls disgrace their parents—it is a bad thing—read the English book and wrote my homework—ate my supper—went to bed at 9 p.m.

August 31, 1982 (Tuesday)

Woke up early in the morning—prepared my school uniform and packed my books—left home at 7:30—caught a taxi—arrived in time for school—took a book in the library—left school—caught a 4 pm bus—prepared my sports clothes—had a bath—ate my supper at 8 p.m.—went to the Peace Society—heard so many cases—they disgusting cases—I realise that blacks are suffering—others are drunkards and burning their houses—all this terrible things—returned home at 11:00—went to bed at 11:30.

September 5, 1982 (Sunday)

Woke up early in the morning—washed myself—ate breakfast—prepared my church clothes—and went to church—after church went home and ate my lunch—phoned my boyfriend and asked him to go to Wits University to watch a dance—and he agreed—we enjoyed the dance very much but what amazed us the most was that there were only 5 blacks—there are so many blacks at the weekend who romp around Soweto—what made me to think about this is that—there are so many boys and girls whom we attended the same Lower Primary—but they've jumped so many stages—they are now mothers and fathers for they have children—they are so small for their stage—they are thugs, thieves and others are drinking alcohol—they don't have any decency.

September 7, 1982 (Tuesday)

Woke up early in the morning—prepared my school uniform—went to school—arrived in time—went to the Debating Society after school—the topic was "World Without Media Would Be Better." I was one of the opposers[;] we argued and argued—and it was late and we closed the meeting—and went home.

September 14, 1982 (Tuesday)

Woke up early in the morning—went to school—arrived in time—enjoy the lessons—caught a 4 p.m. bus—arrived home at 5 p.m.—went to Zone 1 (Meadowlands)—on my way—met some boys—they greeted me—I just passed—they followed me but I was aware of them—I just kept quiet waiting for them to talk—because nowadays if you talk too much they'll kick you—(and) do all those things to you—they asked me to accompany them to where they were going—I asked them whether they didn't see where I was going—one of them said he begged me—I was now getting exasperated—they started to force me—luckily my cousin saw them—he ran towards us—and asked them what they were trying to do—one of them said to my cousin that he was my cousin—my cousin was so angry that he fought them—they ran away—it was a gang of dirty boys and they looked like thugs too—I went to where I was sent and returned home at six o'clock—told my family what had happened—they were sorry—ate my supper—went to bed at 9 p.m.

45

Statement by a Woman Evicted Off a Farm at Weenan, Natal

1980

Without independent communities or even chiefs, workers and labor tenants on white-owned farms could not organize resistance to forced removals, as the Motoks community did (see Document 42). Impoverished and semiliterate, farm workers and labor tenants were without legal recourse or financial resources. A white farmer had almost unchecked authority to do what he pleased with those who lived on his land, regardless of how long they had lived there. The farmer did not have to give reasons for the expulsion of his resident workers and their families, and had no responsibility to find them alternative accommodation. Women and children, in particular, were the most vulnerable. Those expelled wandered from one farm to the next, searching for employment. They might end up in a faraway Bantustan, or in jail, as in the following account.

I have always lived at _____ and my father and my grandfather. I have 6 children. The eldest is about 18, the youngest about 5. My husband deserted us a long time ago. One of my children worked on the farm—a

"Statement by a Woman Evicted Off a Farm at Weenan, Natal," in Laurine Platzky and Cherryl Walker, *The Surplus People: Forced Removals in South Africa* (Johannesburg: Ravan Press, 1985), 136.

boy. He's about 16. He earns R12 a month. The farmer gave us three months' notice. We didn't get a letter. This was before Christmas but we had nowhere to go. So I was arrested with two other women. I was in jail for 6 days. I paid R35 to get out, and am still staying on the farm. We expect to be arrested again at any moment.

7

Ending Apartheid: Reforms and Negotiations

46

P. T. POOVALINGAM

Inaugural Address to President's Council
1981

P. W. Botha, prime minister from 1978 to 1984, then president from 1984 to 1989, sought to co-opt Indian and coloured leaders in his process of "reform." Most coloureds and Indians supported the liberation struggle and refused to collaborate in limited reforms targeted at their own communities instead of at blacks in general. (See Documents 23 and 28.) However, a few anticommunist Indians and coloureds served on an advisory body called the President's Council, which led to the Tricameral Constitution of 1983. This gave coloureds and Indians representation in their own parliamentary bodies within South Africa but limited black African citizenship to the Bantustans. Poovalingam became a member of parliament under this system even as he resigned from the President's Council and denounced the 1983 constitution over the exclusion of Africans. His address also highlights the position of Indians in South African society.

I fully understand, Mr. Chairman, the anger and despair of millions of South Africans. And talking of my own in-group, which is the Indian community in South Africa, I share the anger of the 500 000 South Africans of Indian origin who have themselves suffered directly or whose

P. T. Poovalingam, "President's Council," in *A Documentary History of Indian South Africans,* ed. Surendra Bhana and Bridglal Pachai (Stanford, Calif.: Hoover Institution, 1984), 270–74.

families have suffered vicariously because of the effects of the Group Areas legislation. More than 330 000 South African Indians have been uprooted from their homes. Perfectly good brick and tile dwellings have been bulldozed and reduced to rubble. Long-established schools have been destroyed; churches, temples and mosques now stand stark in areas where previously there were thriving communities. In fact, Mr. Chairman, in large areas where previously there lived Indian South Africans for many generations these areas now have the bombed-out, destroyed appearance that District Six so grotesquely presents in this city of Cape Town today. Communities were wantonly destroyed, often in the most vicious and callous manner. . . . The neighbourhood's mutual respect, the community spirit, the mores that act as social controls and this community feeling takes decades, often generations, to weave into a tapestry. Where people are moved out of established areas they may be re-housed elsewhere, possibly even in better buildings, but the community, that very delicate social organism which, next to the family, is so vital for orderly societal development, that is very strong, yet simultaneously is a fragile thing, is destroyed, and when that happens juvenile delinquency increases, the crime-rate gallops ahead and families fall apart. And I say this with a very heavy heart because for a long time the Indian community in South Africa had the unique distinction of being the most law-abiding group in South Africa. Now that unique distinction is no more. In many new areas of resettlement crime is thriving, juvenile delinquency is terrible, the divorce-rate is climbing. My own in-group thus has and continues to suffer grievously; and salt is rubbed into the wounds when even as late as last week a family which was occupying its ancestral home over successive generations for more than eighty years was told by a state official in writing that that family is committing a criminal offence by remaining on its own property. . . .

. . . We have to face the fact that in our own country there are many things that are considered legal which are quite immoral; and there are many things which are entirely moral but are illegal. Let me say at once that this is not peculiar to our own country for we are fond of saying that our problems are unique. Yet we must remember that the country of my ancestors, my father's homeland—not my homeland, my homeland is the whole of South Africa—my father's homeland, perfected the art of racial discrimination long, long before even Jan van Riebeeck was born. The caste system of India with its numerous barriers against human relations, with its own group areas, its segregationary practices, its equivalent of the Mixed Marriages and Immorality Act laws, existed for centuries. . . . That is what made it possible for India to be conquered. . . . That is what reduced to penury that once great land which was once so rich and so legendary that the world was discovered by Europeans in their quest for India. That land was reduced to its present very sad, sad state because they started with racial discrimination, which corrupted. Caste discrimination, like racial discrimination, corrodes the soul of the doer as well as of the victim; and it is self-destructive. . . . We must recall that truism which has become a cliché, that a house divided falls easy victim. And, Mr. Chairman, there is an enemy almost at our doors. The enemy is neither white, nor black, nor brown; the real enemy is red. The agents of Russian [Soviet] Imperialism have with great skill latched on to the troubles and the problems in our country, and the anguish of so many of our peoples, and the deep discontent that we must acknowledge does exist. . . .

. . . For if the current tentative moves being made for reform fail, or if the minimum hopes that have been raised are not realised, then there will be only one victor, that known as Russian Imperialism.

47

FREDERICK W. DE KLERK

Address to Parliament
February 2, 1990

In September 1989, F. W. de Klerk became president of South Africa, replacing P. W. Botha, whose policies of repression and reform had failed. In this speech to parliament, De Klerk changed the political landscape and made the end of apartheid through negotiations a possibility. He announced a program of political reform, the unbanning of the PAC, ANC, and SACP, and the release of political prisoners, including Nelson Mandela.

The general election [of the white electorate] on September the 6th, 1989, placed our country irrevocably on the road of drastic change. Underlying this is the growing realisation by an increasing number of South Africans

"Appendix B: Address by State President F. W. de Klerk, February 2, 1990," www.sahistory .org.za/archive/address-by-state-president-f-w-de-klerk%2C-dms%2C-at-the-opening-of -the-second-session-of-the-ninth-parliament-of-the-republic-of-south-africa%2C-friday -2-february-1990.

that only a negotiated understanding among the representative leaders of the entire population is able to ensure lasting peace. The alternative is growing violence, tension and conflict. That is unacceptable and in nobody's interest. The well-being of all in this country is linked inextricably to the ability of the leaders to come to terms with one another on a new dispensation. No-one can escape this simple truth. . . .

Practically every leader agrees that negotiation is the key to reconciliation, peace and a new and just dispensation. However, numerous excuses for refusing to take part, are advanced. Some of the reasons being advanced are valid. Others are merely part of [a] political chess game. And while the game of chess proceeds, valuable time is being lost.

Against this background I committed the Government during my inauguration to giving active attention to the most important obstacles in the way of negotiation. Today I am able to announce far-reaching decisions in this connection. I believe that these decisions will shape a new phase in which there will be a movement away from measures which have been seized upon as a justification for confrontation and violence. The emphasis has to move, and will move now, to a debate and discussion of political and economic points of view as part of the process of negotiation. . . .

The steps that have been decided, are the following:

- The prohibition of the African National Congress, the Pan Africanist Congress, the South African Communist Party and a number of subsidiary organisations is being rescinded.

- People serving prison sentences merely because they were members of one of these organisations or because they committed another offence which was merely an offence because of prohibition on one of the organisations was in force, will be identified and released. Prisoners who have been sentenced for other offences such as murder, terrorism or arson are not affected by this.

- The media emergency regulations as well as the education emergency regulations are being abolished in their entirety.

- The security emergency regulations will be amended to still make provision for effective control over visual material pertaining to scenes of unrest.

- The restrictions in terms of the emergency regulations on 33 organisations are being rescinded. The organisations include the following:

National Education Crisis Committee
South African National Students Congress

United Democratic Front
COSATU (Congress of South African Trade Unions)
Blanke Bevrydingsbeweging van Suid-Afrika (White Liberation
Movement).

- The conditions imposed in terms of the security emergency regulations on 374 people on their release, are being rescinded and the regulations which provide for such conditions are being abolished.

- The period of detention in terms of the security emergency regulations will be limited henceforth to six months. Detainees also acquire the right to legal representation and a medical practitioner of their own choosing.

These decisions by the Cabinet are in accordance with the Government's declared intention to normalise the political process in South Africa without jeopardising the maintenance of the good order. They were preceded by thorough and unanimous advice by a group of officials which included members of the security community. . . .

The most important facets of the advice the Government received in this connection, are the following:

- The events in the Soviet Union and Eastern Europe, to which I have referred already, weaken the capability of organisations which were previously supported strongly from those quarters.

- The activities of the organisations from which the prohibitions are now being lifted, no longer entail the same degree of threat to internal security which initially necessitated the imposition of the prohibitions.

- There have been important shifts of emphasis in the statements and points of view of the most important of the organisations concerned, which indicate a new approach and a preference for peaceful solutions.

- The South African Police is convinced that it is able, in the present circumstances, to combat violence and other crimes perpetrated also by members of these organisations and to bring offenders to justice without the aid of prohibitions on organisations.

About one matter there should be no doubt. The lifting of the prohibition on the said organisations does not signify in the least the approval or condonation of terrorism or crimes of violence committed under their banner or which may be perpetrated in the future. Equally, it should not be interpreted as a deviation from the Government's principles, among other things, against their economic policy and aspects of their constitutional policy. This will be dealt with in debate and negotiation. . . . The agenda is open and the overall aims to which we are aspiring should be acceptable to all reasonable South Africans.

Among other things, those aims include a new, democratic constitution; universal franchise; no domination; equality before an independent judiciary; the protection of minorities[1] as well as of individual freedoms; freedom of religion; a sound economy based on proven economic principles and private enterprise; dynamic programmes aimed at better education, health services, housing and social conditions for all.

In this connection Mr Nelson Mandela could play an important part. The Government has noted that he declared himself to be willing to make a constructive contribution to the peaceful political process in South Africa.

I wish to put it plainly that the Government has taken a firm decision to release Mr Mandela unconditionally. . . .

These facts place everybody in South Africa before a fait accompli. On the basis of numerous previous statements there is no longer any reasonable excuse for the continuation of violence. The time for talking has arrived and whoever still makes excuses does not really wish to talk.

[1]In South Africa, "minorities" typically referred to white South Africans.

48

NELSON MANDELA

Speech upon His Release from Prison

February 11, 1990

Upon his release from prison, Nelson Mandela was already in preliminary negotiations with F. W. de Klerk—what Mandela and the ANC termed "negotiations about negotiations." Given the emotional intensity of the

"Speech by Nelson Mandela on the Grand Parade, Cape Town, February 11, 1990," in Gail M. Gerhart and Clive L. Glaser, *From Protest to Challenge: A Documentary History of African Politics in South Africa, 1882–1990*, vol. 6, *Challenge and Victory, 1980–1990* (Bloomington: Indiana University Press, 2010), 725–28.

day, Mandela delivered a formal and scripted speech in which he care-
fully defined his own position in relation to the ANC, reiterated the need
for struggle in addition to negotiations, and insisted on a unified and
democratic South Africa.

Amandla! Amandla! iAfrika Mayibuye! [Power! Power! Let Africa come back!]

Friends, comrades, and fellow South Africans. I greet you all in the name of peace, democracy and freedom for all. I stand here before you not as a prophet but as a humble servant of you, the people. Your tireless and heroic sacrifices have made it possible for me to be here today. I therefore place the remaining years of my life in your hands.

On this day of my release, I extend my sincere and warmest gratitude to the millions of my compatriots and those in every corner of the globe who have campaigned tirelessly for my release.

I send special greetings to the people of Cape Town, this city which has been my home for three decades. Your mass marches and other forms of struggle have served as a constant source of strength to all political prisoners. . . .

Today the majority of South Africans, black and white, recognise that apartheid has no future. It has to be ended by our own decisive mass action in order to build peace and security. The mass campaign of defiance and other actions of our organisation and people can only culminate in the establishment of democracy. The destruction caused by apartheid on our subcontinent is incalculable. The fabric of family life of millions of my people has been shattered. Millions are homeless and unemployed. Our economy lies in ruins and our people are embroiled in political strife.

Our resort to the armed struggle in 1960 with the formation of the military wing of the ANC, Umkhonto we Sizwe, was a purely defensive action against the violence of apartheid. The factors which necessitated the armed struggle still exist today. We have no option but to continue. We express the hope that a climate conducive to a negotiated settlement will be created soon so that there may no longer be the need for the armed struggle.

I am a loyal and disciplined member of the African National Congress. I am therefore in full agreement with all of its objectives, strategies and tactics. The need to unite the people of our country is as important a task now as it always has been. No individual leader is able to take on this enormous task on his own. It is our task as leaders to place our views before our organisation and to allow the democratic structures to decide.

On the question of democratic practice, I feel duty bound to make the point that a leader of the movement is a person who has been democratically elected at a national conference. This is a principle which must be upheld without any exceptions.

Today I wish to report to you that my talks with the government have been aimed at normalising the political situation in the country. We have not as yet begun discussing the basic demands of the struggle. I wish to stress that I myself have at no time entered into negotiations about the future of our country except to insist on a meeting between the ANC and the government.

Mr. de Klerk has gone further than any other Nationalist president in taking real steps to normalise the situation. However, there are further steps as outlined in the Harare Declaration that have to be met before negotiations on the basic demands of our people can begin. I reiterate our call for, *inter alia*, the immediate ending of the State of Emergency and the freeing of all, and not only some, political prisoners. Only such a normalised situation, which allows for free political activity, can allow us to consult our people in order to obtain a mandate. The people need to be consulted on who will negotiate and on the content of such negotiations.

Negotiations cannot take place above the heads or behind the backs of our people. It is our belief that the future of our country can only be determined by a body which is democratically elected on a nonracial basis. Negotiations on the dismantling of apartheid will have to address the overwhelming demand of our people for a democratic, nonracial, and unitary South Africa. There must be an end to white monopoly on political power and a fundamental restructuring of our political and economic systems to ensure that the inequalities of apartheid are addressed and our society thoroughly democratised.

It must be added that Mr. de Klerk himself is a man of integrity who is acutely aware of the dangers of a public figure not honouring his undertakings. But as an organisation we base our policy and strategy on the harsh reality we are faced with. And this reality is that we are still suffering under the policy of the Nationalist government. Our struggle has reached a decisive moment. We call on our people to seize this moment so that the process towards democracy is rapid and uninterrupted. We have waited too long for our freedom. We can no longer wait. Now is the time to intensify the struggle on all fronts. To relax our efforts now would be a mistake which generations to come will not be able to forgive. The sight of freedom looming on the horizon should encourage us to redouble our efforts. It is only through disciplined mass action that our victory can be assured.

We call on our white compatriots to join us in the shaping of a new South Africa. The freedom movement is a political home for you, too. We call on the international community to continue the campaign to isolate the apartheid regime. To lift sanctions now would be to run the risk of aborting the process towards the complete eradication of apartheid. Our march to freedom is irreversible. We must not allow fear to stand in our way. Universal suffrage on a common voters role in a united, democratic, and nonracial South Africa is the only way to peace and racial harmony.

49

MONDLI MAKHANYA

A Tough Guy Is Moved to Tears

1994

In 1994, after four years of fraught negotiations, the first multiparty elections were held under a negotiated constitution and universal franchise. Elections were a restoration of human dignity for black South Africans — an emotional and almost spiritual experience. In this newspaper column, Mondli Makhanya, who would become a prominent journalist and editor, expresses his exhilaration but remains wary of the commitment of the ANC to its key constituency, disempowered blacks.

I like to think I'm a tough guy, the type that only cries at family funerals. But on Wednesday, alone in my voting cubicle, tears clouded my eyes as I held that piece of paper in my hand.

This was not just a vote. It was a spiritual experience. Like the octogenarians who had cast their votes the day before, I felt my humanity had been restored.

I made my cross next to the picture of Nelson Mandela, a man who just a few years ago I could only sing about and whose photographs I

Mondli Makhanya, "A Tough Guy Is Moved to Tears," *Weekly Mail & Guardian*, April 29– May 5, 1994.

used to hide at the bottom of the family deep-freeze. As I put my ballots in the boxes I almost suffocated with emotion as I realized the sanctity of the act I was performing. Together with millions of my black countrymen I was completing a journey that began more than three centuries ago when the white man landed in the Cape and proceeded to strip away my humanity.

This was the end of my nightmare.

As I drove away from Guguletu's Uluntu Centre—where Archbishop Desmond Tutu had earlier cast off his chains—I recalled the emotions of the previous night, when I watched the death of the flag that symbolised all that was cruel and evil to me. In the privacy of the car, under cover of night, I wept.

The man I voted for is not perfect, but human like me. The party I voted for is even further from perfection. Yet he is the one millions of blacks around the country feel they can trust with the task of making a difference in their lives. Those millions of people, from Babanango to Seshego, who put their votes in the same square as myself did not do so flippantly: They, like myself, have hopes and dreams they believe only the ANC can address.

And those dreams and hopes are far from the racist stereotypes of black expectations—such as BMWs and mansions for all of us. The people who voted this week are realistic. All they want are ordinary things like jobs, decent living conditions and a good education for their children.

The challenge for the ANC is not to forget those people as parliamentarians become the new elite, moving into parliamentary villages and white suburbia and enjoying the perks that come with the job.

It will be easy to forget the blacks when the call for reconciliation and fear of a white exodus inevitably conflict with the need to improve the lives of the poor. It will be easy to forget the "natives" out there on the periphery when the power of lobbying rests in lily-white boardrooms and the holiday homes of white executives. It will be easy to forget when the ANC's fear of alienating its growing white support base compromises its ability to satisfy the wishes of those the ANC set out to liberate 80 years ago. It will also be easy to forget when the umbilical cord of struggle is broken and the ANC is the ruler whom the people blame for their misery. If any of this were to happen, the many tears shed this week would be shed again.

But this time they would be tears of sadness and anger at the betrayal of our trust.

50

S. FRANCIS, H. DUGMORE, AND RICO

Madam & Eve: Free at Last

1994

Madam & Eve *was a political cartoon published in the liberal newspaper the* Weekly Mail *(from 1995 called the* Mail & Guardian*). Against the backdrop of current affairs, the cartoon strip expressed the domestic labor relations typical of many white households that employed black men and women for domestic work, as indicated in Document 37. The strip in this selection, published in 1994, reveals the limits of political enfranchisement for economically disempowered black South Africans.*

S. Francis & Rico, Rapid Phase—2016.

A Chronology of Key Events in the Rise and Fall of Apartheid (1652–1994)

1652 Dutch East India Company official Jan van Riebeeck establishes settlement on the Cape; later celebrated as founder of white South Africa.

1806 British seize Cape Colony; beginning of British settlement.

1899–1902 Anglo-Boer War: Boer (Dutch) republics of Transvaal and Orange Free State against British Empire.

1910 Union of South Africa founded, including Cape Colony, Natal, Transvaal, and Orange Free State; Louis Botha and Jan Smuts lead country.

1912 South African Native National Congress formed; precursor of African National Congress (ANC).

1913 Natives Land Act passed.

1924 J. B. M. Hertzog's National Party wins election; Hertzog becomes prime minister.

1934 Hertzog and Smuts form United Party. D. F. Malan forms Gesuiwerde (Purified) National Party.

1939 South Africa enters World War II on side of the Allies.

Hertzog breaks with Smuts and resigns as prime minister; Smuts becomes prime minister.

1940 Hertzog joins Malan's new Herenigde (Reunited) National Party.

1944 ANC Youth League founded.

1948 Malan's National Party wins general election with apartheid policy.

1950–1959 Key apartheid legislation passed.

1952 Defiance Campaign led by the ANC.

1955 Congress of the People meets and proclaims Freedom Charter.

1955–
1959   Destruction of Sophiatown and forced removals to Soweto.

1956–
1961   Treason trial of anti-apartheid activists; defendants acquitted in 1961.

1958   Hendrik F. Verwoerd becomes prime minister.

1959   Robert Sobukwe's Pan Africanist Congress (PAC) splits from ANC and initiates anti-pass campaign.

1960   Massacre of sixty-nine anti-pass protesters at Sharpeville. State of emergency declared; ANC and PAC banned; launch of Umkhonto we Sizwe (MK).

1961   Declaration of Republic of South Africa and withdrawal from British Commonwealth.

1962   Nelson Mandela captured.

1963   MK leaders captured at farm in Rivonia, near Johannesburg.

1963–
1964   Rivonia Trial; Mandela and other defendants found guilty and imprisoned for life.

1966   Verwoerd assassinated; B. J. (John) Vorster becomes prime minister.

1967   Albert Lutuli dies in train accident; Oliver Tambo becomes head of ANC.

1968–
1982   Destruction of District Six and forced removal to Cape Flats.

1975   Angola and Mozambique become independent; provide opportunities for MK exiles to infiltrate South Africa.

1976   Protests against Bantu Education lead to Soweto uprising.

1977   Black Consciousness leader Stephen Bantu Biko killed in detention.

1978   P. W. Botha becomes prime minister.

1982   Internal Security Act provides sweeping powers for police to act against anti-apartheid activists.

1983   United Democratic Front (UDF) unifies internal anti-apartheid groups.

1984   P. W. Botha becomes president of South Africa under Tricameral Constitution.

1984–
1990   Urban uprisings against apartheid peak.

1985   Congress of South African Trade Unions (COSATU) formed. KAIROS places churches on side of the oppressed.

**1985–
1986** Reversal of some apartheid measures, including petty apartheid and pass laws.

**1987–
1988** Battle of Cuito Cuanavale in southern Angola leads to South Africa's withdrawal from Angola and Namibia's independence from South Africa.

1989 Botha suffers stroke; F. W. de Klerk becomes head of National Party and president of South Africa.

1990 De Klerk lifts ban on political organizations and promises to release political prisoners; Nelson Mandela and many other political prisoners freed.

**1990–
1994** Negotiations lead to post-apartheid South Africa.

1994 *April 27* First democratic elections in South Africa.

Questions for Consideration

1. Considering Documents 1, 2, and 3, why was the Natives Land Act of 1913 such an important precursor of apartheid?

2. Compare the segregationist ideas of Jan Smuts and the policies of apartheid outlined by P. O. Sauer and developed by Hendrik F. Verwoerd (Documents 4, 6, 8, and 9). In what ways are they similar and different?

3. Discuss the basis of "grand apartheid" (Documents 9, 11, and 12). How does it differ from "petty apartheid" (Documents 9 and 10) and the Jim Crow laws of the U.S. South?

4. Using Documents 4, 5, 6, 12, 36, and 37, discuss white South African paternalism regarding black South Africans.

5. Based on the documents in chapters 2 and 6, compare apartheid with other forms of institutionalized discrimination and statutory racism you have studied—for example, Jim Crow laws, German Nazism, and Israeli Zionism.

6. Consider the influence of Christianity on the liberation movements through the writings of Albert Lutuli, the ANC national anthem, and the KAIROS declaration (Documents 16, 19, and 30).

7. How did the principles of the Freedom Charter (Document 17) challenge those of apartheid?

8. Compare the different ideologies of resistance: the nonracialism of the Freedom Charter, the Africanism of the PAC, and Black Consciousness.

9. Use the documents in chapters 3, 4, and 5 to describe the motivations and consequences of the ANC's adoption of the armed struggle. Was it effective compared with other strategies of resistance?

10. The photograph of Hector Pieterson (Document 26) became a rallying point for anti-apartheid activism. With reference to documents in chapters 4 and 5, discuss why this photo was so powerful.

11. Using the documents in chapter 5, discuss the tactics of repression used by the apartheid state and their efficacy.

12. Discuss Derek Bauer's caricature of P. W. Botha (Document 31) as a reflection of the broader white attitudes revealed in Documents 32, 33, 34, and 38.

13. How did the other forms of resistance described in chapter 5, such as the student uprisings of 1976, worker movements, and the women's emancipation struggle, relate to the opposition to apartheid led by the ANC?

14. Describe the representation of forced removals in Documents 40, 41, 42, and 45.

15. Use Documents 28, 36, 43, 44, and 45 to discuss the triple oppression of women as workers, as blacks, and as women.

16. South African society is usually perceived as divided between black and white. Choose and discuss documents that complicate this view.

17. Consider the use of the Truth and Reconciliation Commission testimonies of victims of apartheid (Documents 20, 33, and 35) as forms of historical evidence. What are the advantages and disadvantages? Do the same advantages and disadvantages appear when considering the testimonies of perpetrators (Documents 32 and 34)?

18. Compare F. W. de Klerk's February 1990 speech (Document 47) with Nelson Mandela's speech upon his release from prison in the same month (Document 48). What difficulties did they face going into negotiations?

19. What misgivings are expressed by Mondli Makhanya and the contemporaneous *Madam & Eve* cartoon regarding the 1994 elections (Documents 49 and 50)?

Selected Bibliography

GENERAL HISTORIES

Beinart, William. *Twentieth-Century South Africa*. Oxford: Oxford University Press, 1994.

Clark, Nancy, and William Worger. *South Africa: The Rise and Fall of Apartheid*. London: Pearson Longman, 2004.

Davenport, T. R. H., and Christopher Saunders. *South Africa: A Modern History*. 5th ed. London: Macmillan, 2000.

Ross, Robert, Anne Mager, and Bill Nasson, eds. *The Cambridge History of South Africa*. Vol. 2, *1885–1994*. Cambridge: Cambridge University Press, 2011.

Thomson, Leonard. *A History of South Africa*. New Haven, Conn.: Yale University Press, 2001.

Worden, Nigel. *The Making of Modern South Africa*. 5th ed. Sussex: John Wiley & Sons, 2012.

WEB-BASED SOURCES

Nelson Mandela Digital Archive Project, http://archive.nelsonmandela.org/home.

South African History Archive, www.saha.org.za.

South African History Online, www.sahistory.org.za.

PRECURSORS

Dubow, Saul. *Racial Segregation and the Origins of Apartheid in South Africa*. London: Macmillan, 1989.

Du Toit, André. "No Chosen People: The Myth of the Calvinist Origins of Afrikaner Nationalism and Racial Ideology." *American Historical Review* 88, no. 4 (1983).

Du Toit, Marijke. "The Domesticity of Afrikaner Nationalism: *Volksmoeders* and the ACVV, 1904–1929." *Journal of Southern African Studies* 29 (2003): 155–76.

Furlong, Patrick. *Between Crown and Swastika: The Impact of the Radical Right on the Afrikaner Nationalist Movement*. Hanover, N.H.: University Press of New England, 1991.

Higginson, John. *Collective Violence and the Agrarian Origins of South African Apartheid, 1900–1948.* Cambridge: Cambridge University Press, 2014.

Moodie, Dunbar. *The Rise of Afrikanerdom.* Berkeley: University of California Press, 1976.

Nasson, William. *The War for South Africa: The Anglo-Boer War, 1899–1902.* Cape Town: Tafelberg, 2010.

O'Meara, Dan. *Volkskapitalisme: Class, Capital and Ideology in the Development of Afrikaner Nationalism.* Cambridge: Cambridge University Press, 1983.

Rich, Paul. *White Power and the Liberal Conscience: Racial Segregation and South African Liberalism.* Johannesburg: Ravan Press, 1984.

Swanson, Maynard. "The Sanitation Syndrome: Bubonic Plague and Urban Native Policy in the Cape Colony." *Journal of African History* 18 (1977): 387–410.

Trapido, Stanley. "South Africa in a Comparative Study of Industrialization." *Journal of Development Studies* 7, no. 3 (1971): 309–20.

THE IDEOLOGY AND FUNCTIONING OF APARTHEID

Adam, Heribert. *Modernizing Racial Domination.* Berkeley: University of California Press, 1971.

Breckenridge, Keith. *Biometric State: The Global Politics of Identification and Surveillance in South Africa, 1850–Present.* Cambridge: Cambridge University Press, 2014.

Dubow, Saul. *Apartheid, 1948–1994.* Oxford: Oxford University Press, 2014.

Giliomee, Hermann. *The Afrikaners: Biography of a People.* Cape Town: Tafelberg, 2003.

Maré, Gerald, and Georgina Hamilton. *An Appetite for Power: Buthelezi's Inkatha and South Africa.* Johannesburg: Ravan Press, 1987.

O'Meara, Dan. *Forty Lost Years: The Apartheid State and the Politics of the National Party, 1948–1994.* Johannesburg: Ravan Press, 1997.

Posel, Deborah. *The Making of Apartheid, 1948–1961.* New York: Oxford University Press, 1991.

Southall, Roger. *South Africa's Transkei: The Political Economy of an "Independent" Bantustan.* London: Heinemann, 1982.

Witz, Leslie. *Apartheid's Festivals: Contesting South Africa's National Pasts.* Bloomington: Indiana University Press, 2003.

Wolpe, Harold. *Race, Class, and the Apartheid State.* London: James Currey, 1988.

DEFIANCE: CREATING A LIBERATION MOVEMENT

Bradford, Helen. *A Taste of Freedom: The ICU in Rural South Africa, 1924–1930.* New Haven, Conn.: Yale University Press, 1987.

Gerhardt, Gail. *Black Power in South Africa: The Evolution of an Ideology.* Berkeley: University of California Press, 1978.

Lodge, Tom. *Black Politics in South Africa since 1945*. London: Longman, 1983.

Mandela, Nelson. *Long Walk to Freedom: The Autobiography of Nelson Mandela*. New York: Little, Brown, 1994.

Marks, Shula, and Stanley Trapido. *The Politics of Race, Class, and Nationalism in Twentieth-Century South Africa*. London: Longman, 1987.

Meli, Francis. *South Africa Belongs to Us: A History of the ANC*. London: James Currey, 1989.

Odendaal, André. *Vukani Bantu: The Beginnings of Black Protest Politics in South Africa to 1912*. Cape Town: David Philip, 1981.

Roux, Edward. *Time Longer Than Rope: A History of the Black Man's Struggle for Freedom in South Africa*. London: Gollancz, 1948.

Walshe, Peter. *The Rise of African Nationalism in South Africa*. London: C. Hurst, 1978.

VIOLENCE AND ARMED STRUGGLE

Baines, Gary. *South Africa's "Border War": Contested Narratives and Conflicting Memories*. New York: Bloomsbury, 2014.

Buntman, Fran. *Robben Island and Prisoner Resistance to Apartheid*. Cambridge: Cambridge University Press, 2003.

Cherry, Janet. *Spear of the Nation: Umkhonto we Sizwe; South Africa's Liberation Struggle*. Athens: Ohio University Press, 2012.

Cock, Jacklyn, and Laurie Nathan, eds. *War and Society: The Militarisation of South Africa*. Cape Town: David Philip, 1989.

Dlamini, Jacob. *Askari: A Story of Collaboration and Betrayal in the Anti-Apartheid Struggle*. Oxford: Jacana Media, 2015.

Ellis, Stephen. *External Mission: The ANC in Exile, 1960–1990*. London: Hurst, 2012.

Ellis, Stephen, and Tsepo Sechaba. *Comrades against Apartheid*. London: James Currey, 1992.

Lodge, Tom. *Sharpeville: An Apartheid Massacre and Its Consequences*. New York: Oxford University Press, 2011.

Maloka, Eddy. *The South African Communist Party in Exile, 1963–1990*. Cape Town: Africa Institute, 2002.

Truth and Reconciliation Commission. *Truth and Reconciliation Commission of South Africa Report*. 5 vols. Cape Town: Juta, 1998.

RESISTANCE AND REPRESSION: STUDENTS, WORKERS, WOMEN, CLERGY, AND CONSCRIPTS

Baskin, Jeremy. *Striking Back: A History of COSATU*. Johannesburg: Ravan Press, 1991.

Bozzoli, Belinda. *Theatres of Struggle and the End of Apartheid*. Athens: Ohio University Press, 2004.

Cobbet, William, and Robin Cohen, eds. *Popular Struggles in South Africa*. London: James Currey, 1988.

Glaser, Clive. *Ba-Tsotsi: The Youth Gangs of Soweto, 1935–1976*. Portsmouth, N.H.: Heinemann, 2000.

Hirson, Baruch. *Year of Fire, Year of Ash: The Soweto Revolt; Roots of a Revolution?* London: Zed, 1979.

Landau, Paul. *Popular Politics in the History of South Africa*. Cambridge: Cambridge University Press, 2010.

Magaziner, Dan. *The Law and the Prophets: Black Consciousness in South Africa, 1968–1977*. Athens: Ohio University Press, 2010.

Pityana, Barney, Mamphele Ramphele, Malusi Mpunlwana, and Lindy Wilson, eds. *Bounds of Possibility: The Legacy of Steve Biko and Black Consciousness*. London: Zed, 1991.

Seekings, Jeremy. *The UDF: A History of the United Democratic Front in South Africa, 1983–1991*. Athens: Ohio University Press, 2000.

Walker, Cherryl. *Women and Resistance in South Africa*. London: Onyx, 1982.

LIVING WITH APARTHEID: CLASS, RACE, AND GENDER

Adhikiri, Mohammad. *Not White Enough, Not Black Enough: Racial Identity in the South African Coloured Community*. Athens: Ohio University Press, 2005.

Beinart, William, and Colin Bundy. *Hidden Struggles in Rural South Africa: Politics and Popular Movements in the Transkei and Eastern Cape, 1890–1930*. Johannesburg: Ravan Press, 1987.

Bozzoli, Belinda, ed. *Class, Community, Conflict: South African Perspectives*. Johannesburg: Ravan Press, 1987.

———. "Marxism, Feminism, and South African Studies." *Journal of Southern African Studies* 9, no. 2 (1983): 139–71.

Bozzoli, Belinda, and Mmantho Nkotsoe. *Women of Phokeng: Consciousness, Life Strategy, and Migrancy in South Africa, 1900–1983*. Johannesburg: Ravan Press, 1991.

Bundy, Colin. *The Rise and Fall of the South African Peasantry*. 2nd ed. London: Heinemann, 1988.

Cock, Jacklyn. *Maids and Madams: A Study in the Politics of Exploitation*. Johannesburg: Ravan Press, 1980.

Coplan, David. *In Township Tonight! South Africa's Black City Music and Theatre*. Johannesburg: Ravan Press, 1985.

Crais, Clifton. *The Politics of Evil: Magic, State Power, and the Political Imagination in South Africa*. Cambridge: Cambridge University Press, 2002.

Dlamini, Jacob. *Native Nostalgia*. Johannesburg: Jacana Media, 2010.

Freund, William. *Insiders and Outsiders: The Indian Working Class of Durban, 1910–1990*. Portsmouth, N.H.: Heinemann, 1995.

Jacobs, Nancy. *Environment, Power, and Injustice: A South African History*. Cambridge: Cambridge University Press, 2003.

Jeeves, Alan. *Migrant Labour in South Africa's Mining Economy: The Struggle for the Gold Mines' Labour Supply, 1890–1920*. Johannesburg: Witwatersrand University Press, 1985.

Johnstone, Frederick. *Class, Race, and Gold: A Study of Class Relations and Racial Discrimination in South Africa*. London: Routledge, 1976.

Kallaway, Peter, ed. *A History of Education under Apartheid*. Cape Town: Maskew Miller Longman, 2002.

Keegan, Tim. *Rural Transformations in Industrializing South Africa: The Southern Highveld to 1914*. London: Macmillan, 1987.

Mager, Anne. *Beer, Sociability, and Masculinity in South Africa*. Bloomington: Indiana University Press, 2010.

————. *Gender and the Making of a South African Bantustan: A Social History of the Ciskei, 1945–1959*. Portsmouth, N.H.: Heinemann, 1999.

Marks, Shula, and Richard Rathbone, eds. *Industrialisation and Social Change in South Africa*. London: Longman, 1982.

Moodie, Dunbar, and Vivienne Ndatshe. *Going for Gold: Men, Mines, and Migration*. Berkeley: University of California Press, 1994.

Morrell, Robert, ed. *Changing Men in South Africa*. Pietermaritzburg: University of Kwazulu-Natal Press, 2001.

Platzky, Laurine, and Cherryl Walker. *The Surplus People: Forced Removals in South Africa*. Johannesburg: Ravan Press, 1985.

Van Onselen, Charles. *The Seed Is Mine: The Life of Kas Maine, a South African Sharecropper, 1894–1985*. Cape Town: David Philip, 1996.

————. *Studies in the Social and Economic History of the Witwatersrand*. Vols. 1 and 2. London: Longman, 1982.

Western, John. *Outcast Cape Town*. 2nd ed. Berkeley: University of California Press, 1996.

Wilson, Francis, and Mamphele Ramphele. *Uprooting Poverty: The South African Challenge*. New York: W. W. Norton, 1989.

ENDING APARTHEID: REFORMS AND NEGOTIATIONS

Davenport, T. R. H. *The Transfer of Power in South Africa*. Toronto: University of Toronto Press, 1998.

Waldmeir, Patti. *Anatomy of a Miracle: The End of Apartheid and the Birth of a New South Africa*. New York: W. W. Norton, 1997.

Acknowledgments (*continued from p. iv*)

Document 5: Gerhardus Eloff, *Rasse en rassevermenging, die boerevolk gesien van die standpunt van die rasseleer* (Bloemfontein: Nasionale Pers, 1942), 101–4. Translated by David Gordon.

Document 6: *Verslag van die Kleurvraagstuk-Kommissie van die Herenigde Nasionale Party* (1947), 1–16. Abridged and translated by David Gordon.

Document 7: "History Comes to Life," *Cape Times*, April 4, 1952, p. 5. Reprinted by permission of the National Library of South Africa.

Document 19: Albert Lutuli, Nobel Lecture: Africa and Freedom. Nobelprize.org. Nobel Media AB, December 11, 1961. Copyright © The Nobel Foundation, 1961. Used with permission.

Document 21: Nelson R. Mandela, "Statement during the Rivonia Trial," in *From Protest to Challenge: A Documentary History of African Politics in South Africa*, Vol. 3: *Challenge and Violence, 1953–1964* (Stanford, Calif.: Hoover Institute, 1977), 771–96. Reprinted by permission of the Nelson Mandela Foundation.

Document 23: Dennis Brutus, *A Simple Lust* (Heinemann, 1973). Reprinted by permission of Antony M. Brutus.

Document 24: Oliver R. Tambo, "A Future Free of Exploitation, 1977." Excerpted from "Address to the First Congress of the MPLA, December 1977," in Sechaba, April–June 1978. Reprinted with permission from the African National Congress.

Document 25: Stephen Bantu Biko, "The Definition of Black Consciousness," in *I Write What I Like*. Copyright © 1978 N. M. Biko. Reprinted by permission of Pan Macmillan South Africa.

Document 28: Frene Ginwala, "ANC Women: Their Strength in the Struggle," *Work in Progress* (*WIP*) 45, November 1986. pp. 10–11, 14. Reprinted by permission of Frene Ginwala.

Document 30: *A Challenge to the Church: A Theological Comment on the Political Crisis in South Africa* (Braamfontein: Skotaville Publishers, 1985). Abridged. Reprinted by permission of Skotaville Publishers/Mutloatse Arts Heritage Trust.

Document 36: Shula Marks, ed., *"Not Either an Experimental Doll": The Separate Worlds of Three South African Women* (Pietermartizburg: University of Natal Press, 1987), 68–81. Reprinted by permission of Shula Marks.

Document 39: From "Amagoduka at Glencoe Station." Mbuyiseni Oswald Mtshali, *Sounds of a Cowhide Drum*. © Mbuyiseni Oswald Mtshali, 2012. Jacana Media (Pty) Ltd. Reprinted by permission.

Document 42: Interview with Member of the Community, Matoks Location, Bandelierkop (1979). From "Communities in Crisis – Six Case Studies," in *The Surplus People: Forced Removals in South Africa*, Laurine Platzky and Cherryl Walker (Johannesburg: Ravan Press, 1985), 250–55. Reprinted by permission of Dr. Laurine Platzky.

Document 43: Emma Mashinini, *Strikes Have Followed Me All My Life* (New York: Routledge, 1991. Orig. London: The Women's Press, 1989), 14–16. Reprinted by permission of the author.

Document 44: Mbuyiseni Oswald Mtshali, *Give Us a Break: Diaries of a Group of Soweto Children* (Johannesburg: Skotaville, 1988), 60–64. Reprinted by permission of Skotaville Publishers/Mutloatse Arts Heritage Trust.

Document 48: Nelson Mandela, "Speech on His Release from Prison, February 11, 1990." From *Protest to Challenge*, Vol. 6: *Challenge and Victory, 1980–1990*, ed. G. Gerhart and C. Glaser (Bloomington: Indiana University Press, 2010), 725–28. Reprinted by permission of the Nelson Mandela Foundation.

Document 49: Mondli Makhanya, "A Tough Guy Is Moved to Tears," *Mail & Guardian*, 29 April–5 May 1994. Reprinted by permission of the Mail & Guardian.

Index

177